First World War
and Army of Occupation
War Diary
France, Belgium and Germany

66 DIVISION
199 Infantry Brigade
Manchester Regiment
9th Battalion
1 March 1918 - 15 May 1919

WO95/3145/5

The Naval & Military Press Ltd
www.nmarchive.com
Published in association with The National Archives

Published by

The Naval & Military Press Ltd

Unit 10 Ridgewood Industrial Park,

Uckfield, East Sussex,

TN22 5QE England

Tel: +44 (0) 1825 749494

www.naval-military-press.com

www.nmarchive.com

This diary has been reprinted in facsimile from the original. Any imperfections are inevitably reproduced and the quality may fall short of modern type and cartographic standards.

© **Crown Copyright**
Images reproduced by permission of The National Archives, London, England, 2015.

Contents

Document type	Place/Title	Date From	Date To
Heading	WO95/3145/5 9 Battalion Manchester Regiment		
Heading	66th Division 199th Infy Bde 9th Bn Manch. Regt Mar 1918-May 1919 Absorbed 13 Bn Aug 1918 (From 42 Div 126 Bde)		
Heading	198th Brigade 66th Division 9th Battalion Manchester Regiment March 1918 From 42 Div 126 Bde		
Heading	War Diary Vol II March-1918		
War Diary	Hesbecourt	01/03/1918	10/03/1918
War Diary	Hervilly	16/03/1918	21/03/1918
War Diary	Hesbecourt	22/03/1918	25/03/1918
War Diary	Vaoxvillers	26/03/1918	27/03/1918
War Diary	Cayeux	27/03/1918	27/03/1918
War Diary	Aubercourt	28/03/1918	31/03/1918
War Diary	Longeau	31/03/1918	31/03/1918
Operation(al) Order(s)	9th Battn The Manchester Regiment Order No. 4	07/03/1918	07/03/1918
Miscellaneous	App B		
Operation(al) Order(s)	KID Orders No. 6	15/03/1918	15/03/1918
Heading	War Diary 9th Battalion The Manchester Regiment Vol III April, 1918		
War Diary	Pissy	01/04/1918	02/04/1918
War Diary	Bissus-Bussuel	03/04/1918	05/04/1918
War Diary	Hautvillers	06/04/1918	11/04/1918
War Diary	Coulonvillers	12/04/1918	12/04/1918
War Diary	Long	13/04/1918	13/04/1918
War Diary	Millencourt	14/04/1918	14/04/1918
War Diary	Long	14/04/1918	14/04/1918
War Diary	Millencourt	15/04/1918	16/04/1918
War Diary	Le Plessiel	17/04/1918	24/04/1918
War Diary	Setques	24/04/1918	25/04/1918
War Diary	Bellebrune	26/04/1918	30/04/1918
Operation(al) Order(s)	9th Battalion The Manchester Regiment Order No. 67	15/04/1918	15/04/1918
Operation(al) Order(s)	9th Battalion The Manchester Regiment Order No 8	12/04/1918	12/04/1918
Operation(al) Order(s)	9th Battalion The Manchester regiment Details Order No. I	13/04/1918	13/04/1918
Miscellaneous	9th Battalion The Manchester Regiment Training Cadre		
Miscellaneous	9th Battalion The Manchester Regiment. Order No. 74	21/04/1918	21/04/1918
Miscellaneous	9th. Battalion The Manchester Regiment.	21/03/1918	21/03/1918
Heading	War Diary of 9th Battn The Manchester Regiment From May 1st To May 31st Volume IV		
War Diary	Bellebrune	01/05/1918	02/05/1918
War Diary	Brutelles	03/05/1918	10/05/1918
War Diary	Franleu	11/05/1918	25/05/1918
War Diary	Montieres	26/05/1918	29/05/1918
War Diary	Franleu	29/05/1918	31/05/1918
Operation(al) Order(s)	9th Battalion The Manchester Regiment Order No. 79	02/05/1918	02/05/1918
Operation(al) Order(s)	9th Battalion The Manchester Regiment Order No. 12	10/05/1918	10/05/1918
Miscellaneous	Programme Of Training May 20th To 26th May Appendix C		
Miscellaneous	Programme Of Training May 20th To 26th Appendix C		
Miscellaneous	Programme Of Training Lewis Gun.		

Type	Description	Date From	Date To
Operation(al) Order(s)	9th Battalion The Manchester Regiment Order No. 13	25/05/1918	25/05/1918
Operation(al) Order(s)	9th Battalion The Manchester Regt. Order No. 14		
Miscellaneous	Battalion Orders By Lieut-Colonel J.L. Heselton D.S.O., M.C., Cmdg. 9th. Battalion The Manchester Regiment. Appendix G	05/05/1918	05/05/1918
Miscellaneous	Battalion Orders By Lieut-Colonel J.L. Heselton, D.S.O., M.C., Cmdg. 9th. Battalion The Manchester Regiment. Appendix G	06/05/1918	06/05/1918
Miscellaneous	Battalion Orders By Lieut-Colonel J.L. Heselton, D.S.O., M.C., Commanding 9th. Battalion The Manchester Regiment. Appendix G	09/05/1918	09/05/1918
Miscellaneous	Battalion Orders By Lieut-Colonel J.L. Heselton, D.S.O., M.C., Commanding 9th. Battalion The Manchester Regiment. Appendix G	12/05/1918	12/05/1918
Miscellaneous	Battalion Orders By Lieut-Colonel J.L. Heselton, D.S.O., M.C., Commanding 9th. Battalion The Manchester Regiment. Appendix G	13/05/1918	13/05/1918
Miscellaneous	Battalion Orders By Lieut-Colonel J.L. Heselton, D.S.O., M.C., Commanding 9th. Battalion The Manchester Regiment. Appendix G	14/05/1918	14/05/1918
Miscellaneous	Battalion Orders By Lieut-Colonel J.L. Heselton, D.S.O., M.C., Commanding 9th. Battalion The Manchester Regiment. Appendix G	15/05/1918	15/05/1918
Miscellaneous	Battalion Orders By Lieut-Colonel J.L. Heselton, D.S.O., M.C., Commanding 9th. Battalion The Manchester Regiment. Appendix G	16/05/1918	16/05/1918
Miscellaneous	Battalion Orders By Lieut-Colonel J.L. Heselton, D.S.O., M.C., Commanding 9th. Battalion The Manchester Regiment. Appendix G	18/05/1918	18/05/1918
Miscellaneous	Battalion Orders By Lieut-Colonel J.L. Heselton, D.S.O., M.C., Commanding 9th. Battalion The Manchester Regiment. Appendix G	19/05/1919	19/05/1919
Miscellaneous	Battalion Orders By Lieut-Colonel J.L. Heselton, D.S.O., M.C., Commanding 9th. Battalion The Manchester Regiment. Appendix G	20/05/1918	20/05/1918
Miscellaneous	Battalion Orders By Lieut-Colonel J.L. Heselton, D.S.O., M.C., Commanding 9th. Battalion The Manchester Regiment. Appendix G	21/05/1918	21/05/1918
Miscellaneous	Battalion Orders By Lieut-Colonel J.L. Heselton, D.S.O., M.C., Commanding 9th. Battalion The Manchester Regiment. Appendix G	24/05/1918	24/05/1918
Miscellaneous	Battalion Orders By Lieut-Colonel J.L. Heselton, D.S.O., M.C., Commanding 9th. Battalion The Manchester Regiment. Appendix G	29/05/1918	29/05/1918
Miscellaneous	Battalion Orders By Lieut-Colonel J.L. Heselton, D.S.O., M.C., Commanding 9th. Battalion The Manchester Regiment. Appendix G	28/05/1918	28/05/1918
War Diary	Franleu	01/06/1918	05/06/1918
War Diary	Woignarue	06/06/1918	14/06/1918
War Diary	Onival	15/06/1918	18/06/1918
War Diary	Pende	19/06/1918	20/06/1918
War Diary	Hautvillers	21/06/1918	21/06/1918
War Diary	Ivergny	22/06/1918	22/06/1918
War Diary	Pierregot	27/06/1918	30/06/1918
Operation(al) Order(s)	9th Battalion The Manchester Regiment Order No. 15	06/06/1918	06/06/1918

Heading	War Diary of 9th Battalion The Manchester Regt. From 1-7-1918 To 31-7-1918 Vol Vi		
War Diary	Pierregot	01/07/1918	21/07/1918
War Diary	Haudricourt	22/07/1918	31/07/1918
Heading	War Diary Of 13th (S) Bn. Manchester Regt. (1st To 13th August. 1918) 9th Bn. Manchester Regt (14th To 31st August 1918)		
War Diary	Haudricourt	01/08/1918	31/08/1918
Miscellaneous	Appendix No.1 Programme of Training & Work. 5th-11th August.		
Miscellaneous	13th (S) Battalion The Manchester Regiment.	19/08/1918	19/08/1918
Miscellaneous	Appendix No 2 Programme of Training and Work. Aug 12th & 13th 1918.		
Miscellaneous	13th (S) Battn, The Manchester Regt.		
Miscellaneous	Appendix No. 3. Programme of Training and Work August 14th to 16th 1918.		
Miscellaneous	13th Battn. The Manchester Regt.		
Miscellaneous	Appendix No. 4. Programme of Training and Work August 16th to 17th 1918.		
Miscellaneous	9th Battalion The Manchester Regiment		
Miscellaneous	Appendix No. 5. Programme of Training and Work August 19th to 20th 1918.		
Miscellaneous	9th Battalion, Manchester Regiment.	19/08/1918	19/08/1918
Miscellaneous	Appendix No. 6. Programme of Training and Work August 21st to 22nd 1918.		
Miscellaneous	9th Bn. Manchester Regiment	21/08/1918	21/08/1918
Miscellaneous	Appendix No. 7. Programme of Training and Work August 23rd to 24th 1918.		
Miscellaneous	9th Battalion, The Manchester Regiment	23/08/1918	23/08/1918
Miscellaneous	Appendix No. 8. Programme of Training and Work August 26th 1918.		
Miscellaneous	9th Battalion, Manchester Regiment	26/08/1918	26/08/1918
Miscellaneous	Appendix No. 9. Programme of Training and Work August 27th 1918.		
Miscellaneous	9th Battalion, Manchester Regiment.	27/08/1918	27/08/1918
Heading	War Diary of 9th Bn Manchester Regt. From 1st To 30th September 1918 Volume No 4-No 9		
War Diary	Haudricourt	01/09/1918	20/09/1918
War Diary	Penin	21/09/1918	21/09/1918
War Diary	Manin	22/09/1918	30/09/1918
Miscellaneous	Appendix No. 1. Programme of Training-Week ending 7-9-18.		
Miscellaneous	9th Bn. Manchester Regiment	07/09/1918	07/09/1918
Miscellaneous	Appendix No. 2. Programme of Training-Week ending 14-9-18.		
Miscellaneous	9th Bn. Manchester Regiment.	14/09/1918	14/09/1918
Miscellaneous	Appendix No. 3. Programme of Training-Week ending 27-9-18.		
Miscellaneous	9th Bn. Manchester Regiment	21/09/1918	21/09/1918
Miscellaneous	Appendix No. 4. Operation Order No. 1		
Operation(al) Order(s)	Operation Order No. 1 By Lieut Colonel J.F.B. Morrell M.V.O. Commanding 9th Battalion the Manchester Regiment		
Miscellaneous	Appendix No. 5. Operation Order No. 2		

Operation(al) Order(s)	Operation Order No. 2. By Lieut Colonel J.F.B. Morrell M.V.O. Commanding 9th Battalion the Manchester Regt		
Miscellaneous	Appendix No. 6. Pamphlet Dropped From Enemy Planes.		
Miscellaneous	Appendix No. 4. Brigade Scheme.		
Miscellaneous	General Idea		
Miscellaneous	9th. Battn. Manchester Regt.	25/09/1918	25/09/1918
Miscellaneous	Herewith Operation Orders For Scheme Tomorrow		
Miscellaneous	Appendix No. 8. Operation Order No. 3		
Operation(al) Order(s)	Operation Order No. 3 By Lieut Colonel J.F.B. Morrell M.V.O. Commanding 9th Battalion The Manchester Regiment	29/09/1918	29/09/1918
Miscellaneous	Appendix No. 9. Operation Order No. 4		
Miscellaneous	Reference Operation Order No. 4	29/09/1918	29/09/1918
Miscellaneous	Appendix No.10. Operation Order No. 5		
Operation(al) Order(s)	Operation Order No. 5 By Lieut Colonel J.F.B. Morrell M.V.O. Commanding 9th Battalion the Manchester Regt	30/09/1918	30/09/1918
Heading	War Diary of 9th Bn The Manchester Regt. From 1st To 31st October 1918		
War Diary	Proyart	01/10/1918	01/10/1918
War Diary	Maricourt	02/10/1918	03/10/1918
War Diary	Moislains	04/10/1918	05/10/1918
War Diary	Moislans To Templeux-La Fosse	05/10/1918	07/10/1918
War Diary	Reumont	11/10/1918	12/10/1918
War Diary	Maurois	13/10/1918	18/10/1918
War Diary	Le Catead K. 36	19/10/1918	20/10/1918
War Diary	Maurois	20/10/1918	20/10/1918
War Diary	Elincourt	21/10/1918	31/10/1918
Miscellaneous	Appendix No. 1. Operation Order No. 6		
Operation(al) Order(s)	Operation Order Number 6. by Lieut Colonel J.F.B. Morrell M.V.O. Commanding 9th Battalion Manchester Regiment	03/10/1918	03/10/1918
Miscellaneous	Appendix No 2. Operation Order No. 7		
Operation(al) Order(s)	Operation Order No. 7 9th Bn Manchester Regt	04/10/1918	04/10/1918
Miscellaneous	Appendix No.8. Operation Order No. 8		
Operation(al) Order(s)	Operation Order No. 8 By Lieut Colonel J.F.B. Morrell M.V.O.	07/10/1918	07/10/1918
Miscellaneous	Appendix No.4. Description of Operation to 11th October 1918.		
Miscellaneous	9th Bn. The Manchester Regt.	11/10/1918	11/10/1918
Miscellaneous	Appendix No.5. Operation Order No. 9		
Operation(al) Order(s)	Operation Order Number 9.	13/10/1918	13/10/1918
Heading	War Diary of 9th Bn The Manchester Regt. From 1st To 30th November 1918		
War Diary	Elincourt	01/11/1918	01/11/1918
War Diary	Maurois	02/11/1918	02/11/1918
War Diary	Lecateau	03/11/1918	05/11/1918
War Diary	Landrecies	06/11/1918	06/11/1918
War Diary	Maroilles	07/11/1918	07/11/1918
War Diary	Marbaix	08/11/1918	08/11/1918
War Diary	La Tuillerie	09/11/1918	09/11/1918
War Diary	Bas Lieu	10/11/1918	10/11/1918
War Diary	Sivry	11/11/1918	18/11/1918
War Diary	Cerfontaine	18/11/1918	24/11/1918

War Diary	Morville	25/11/1918	30/11/1918
Miscellaneous	Appendix No. 1. Operation Order No. 14		
Operation(al) Order(s)	Operation Order No. 14 By Lieut Colonel J.F.B. Morrell M.V.O. Commanding 9th Battalion the Manchester Regiment	01/11/1918	01/11/1918
Miscellaneous	Appendix No 2. Operation Order No. 15		
Operation(al) Order(s)	Operation Order No. 15 by Lieut Colonel J.F.B. Morrell D.S.O. M.V.O. Commanding 9th Battalion Manchester Regiment	03/11/1918	03/11/1918
Miscellaneous	Appendix No 3. Operation Order No. 16		
Operation(al) Order(s)	Operation Order No. 16 By Lieut Col J.F.B. Morrell M.V.O. Commanding 9th Battn the Manchester Regt	04/11/1918	04/11/1918
Miscellaneous	Appendix No 4. Message man of Le Cateau		
Map	Message Map		
Map	Map		
Miscellaneous	Appendix No 5. Description Operations 10th to 11th Nov 1918		
Miscellaneous	Ref Maps. France Sheet 57A		
Miscellaneous	Appendix No. 5A. Gen Rawlinson's message to 4th army.		
Miscellaneous	Fourth Army, No.G.S 125.		
Miscellaneous	Appendix No 6. Instructions for March to Rhine also Operation Order No. 23 & 24.		
Miscellaneous	Instruction For March To Rhine		
Operation(al) Order(s)	Operation Order No. 23 By Lieut Col J.F.B. Morrell M.V.O. Commanding 9th Battn the Manchester Regt	18/11/1918	18/11/1918
Operation(al) Order(s)	Operation Order No. 24 by Lieut Col J.F.B. Morrell M.V.O. Commanding 9th Battn Manchester Regt		
Miscellaneous	Appendix No. 7. Operation Order No. 25		
Operation(al) Order(s)	Operation Order-Number 25 by Lieut Col J.F.B. Morrell D.S.O. M.V.O. Commanding 9th Battalion Manchester Regiment	17/11/1918	17/11/1918
Miscellaneous	Appendix No. 8. Special Order by Maj Gen H.K. Bethell C.M.G. D.S.O.		
Miscellaneous	Special Order	17/11/1918	17/11/1918
Miscellaneous	Appendix No. 9. Operation Order No. 27		
Operation(al) Order(s)	Operation Order No. 27 by Lieut Col J.F.B. Morrell M.V.O. Commanding 9th Battn Manchester Regt	23/11/1918	23/11/1918
Heading	War Diary of 9th Bn The Manchester Regt. From 1st To 31st December 1918, (Armistice Period) Volume No.4-No.12		
War Diary	Morville	01/12/1918	13/12/1918
War Diary	Dinant	14/12/1918	14/12/1918
War Diary	Hamois	14/12/1918	14/12/1918
War Diary	Huy	15/12/1918	31/12/1918
Miscellaneous	Appendix No. 1. Operation Order No. 28		
Operation(al) Order(s)	Operation Order Number 28 by Lieut Col J.F.B. Morrell D.S.O. M.V.O. Commanding 9th Battalion Manchester Regiment	11/12/1918	11/12/1918
Miscellaneous	March Table Of Accompany Operation Order No. 58	13/12/1918	13/12/1918
Miscellaneous	Appendix No. 2. Programme of Training.		
Miscellaneous	Programme Of Training.	28/12/1918	28/12/1918
Heading	War Diary of 9th Bn The Manchester Regt. From 1st To 31st January 1919 (Armistice Period) Volume No.5-No.1		
War Diary	Huy	01/01/1919	31/01/1919

Miscellaneous	Appendix No. 1. Programme of Training.		
Miscellaneous	9th Battalion Manchester Regiment	25/01/1919	25/01/1919
Miscellaneous	Appendix No. 2. Programme of Training.		
Miscellaneous	Training Programme	01/02/1919	01/02/1919
Heading	War Diary of 9th Bn The Manchester Regt. From 1st To 28th February 1919 (Armistice Period) Volume 5 No. 2		
War Diary	Huy	01/02/1919	14/02/1919
War Diary	Seilles	15/02/1919	28/02/1919
Miscellaneous	Appendix No. 1. Programme of Training Week ending 8-2-19		
Miscellaneous	Amendment To Programme Of Training		
Miscellaneous	Training Programme	08/02/1919	08/02/1919
Miscellaneous	Capt C.D. Walker		
Miscellaneous	Appendix No. 2. Programme of Training Week ending 15-2-19		
Miscellaneous	Training Programme	15/02/1919	15/02/1919
Miscellaneous	Appendix No. 3. Operation Order No 29		
Operation(al) Order(s)	Operation Order No. 29 by Lieut Col J.F.B. Morrell D.S.O. M.V.O. Commanding 9th Battalion Manchester Regiment	13/02/1919	13/02/1919
Heading	War Diary of 9th Bn The Manchester Regt. From 1st To 31st March 1919 (Armistice Period) Volume 5 No.3.		
War Diary	Seilles	01/03/1919	31/03/1919
Heading	War Diary of 9th Bn The Manchester Regt. From 1st April 1919 To 30th April 1919 (Armistice Period) Volume 5 No. 4		
War Diary	Seilles	01/04/1919	30/04/1919
Heading	War Diary of 9th Bn The Manchester Regt. From 1st To 15th May 1919 (Armistice Period) Volume 5. No. 5		
War Diary	Seilles	01/05/1919	07/05/1919
War Diary	Ciney	08/05/1919	15/05/1919

WO/95/3145/5

9 Battalion Manchester Regiment

66TH DIVISION
199TH INFY BDE

9TH BN MANCH. REGT
~~MAR~~ 1918 – MAY 1919

Attached 13th Bn AUG 1918

(FROM 42 DIV 126 BDE)

= 198th Brigade
66th Division.

9th BATTALION

MANCHESTER REGIMENT

MARCH 1918

FROM 42 DIV. 126 BDE

CONFIDENTIAL

9th Bn. Manchester Regt.

WAR DIARY

VOL. II

MARCH – 1918

Army Form C. 2118.

WAR DIARY
or
INTELLIGENCE SUMMARY.
(Erase heading not required.)

Instructions regarding War Diaries and Intelligence Summaries are contained in F. S. Regs. Part II. and the Staff Manual respectively. Title pages will be prepared in manuscript.

Place	Date	Hour	Summary of Events and Information	Remarks and references to Appendices
HERBECOURT	1/3/18 to 7/3/18		During these days the Battalion was in Support before Lieu, which was held by 2/5 Pr East Lancashire Regt. The line was quiet during this period.	
	8/3/18		On the 8th the Battalion relieved the 2/5 East Lancashire Regt in the front line of the Corke Triangle in the HARGICOURT Sector.	
	9/3/18			
	10/3/18		On this date 2/Lt H Bowen and 12 men attempted to raid the enemy but owing to the wire being uncut they were unable to enter the German trenches. During the tour in the line the enemy was quiet.	
	16/3/18		On this date the Battalion was relieved by 4/5 R East Lancashire Regiment and went into Reserve at HERVILLY	
HERVILLY	21/3/18		On this morning at 4.30 a.m. the Battalion was ordered to Battle Positions owing to enemy activity. There was clear through strong bombardment which caused about 30 casualties. The Battalion went into action and continued in action till April 5th.	

WAR DIARY
INTELLIGENCE SUMMARY.
(Erase heading not required.)

Place	Date	Hour	Summary of Events and Information	Remarks and references to Appendices
VERMAND	22/3/18		On the 22nd of March the Battalion was in the Red line when it was attacked and beat off another enemy attack. The Battalion had got decided and was withdrawn and Concentrated at BEAUMETZ. On this date Lieut-Colonel E.C. LLOYD	9th Manchester Being the 24th March 1918 "On the morning of 25th" shall not have been returned into 24th. It was on the 25th. A.M. Davies 15.10.26
	23/3/18		From BEAUMETZ the Battalion marched through PERONNE and position on the E. side of the SOMME at ETERPIGNY and covered the withdrawal of another Division over the river when we blew up the bridges. The Battalion was relieved and took over small the enemy.	
	24/3/18		BIACHES. On the morning of 24th the enemy got across the river and in Battalion was forced to withdraw to FOUCAUCOURT. Here the VERMICOURT - ASSEVILLERS line was known.	
	25/3/18		Concentrated in DEMPIERE and marched to FOUCAUCOURT. Here the Battalion again took up a position astride AMIENS - PERONNE road and fought a rear guard action to the FRAMERVILLE - VAUVILLERS line	

INTELLIGENCE SUMMARY.

(Erase heading not required.)

Place	Date	Hour	Summary of Events and Information	Remarks and references to Appendices
HEBECOURT	22/3/18		On the 22nd of March the Battalion retired BACK and when it open took up a position and held off another enemy attack. At the time the Battalion had got scattered and was withdrawn and again to Bn central at BEAUMETZ. On the 23rd Lieut-Colonel E. X. LLOYD D.S.O. was wounded	
	23/3/18		From PERONNE the Battalion marched through PERONNE and took up a position on the E. side of SOMME at ETERPIGNY and covered the retirement of another Division over the river. When we blew up the bridge in the evening the Battalion was relieved and took over another position at BIACHES. On the morning of 24th the Enemy got across here again.	
X	24/3/18		right and in the Battalion was forced to withdraw to the evening to HERBICOURT, ASSEVILLIERS. Was after having been in action the Battalion	
	25/3/18		Concentrated in DOMPIERRE and marched to FOUCAUCOURT. Here the Battalion again took up a position astride AMIENS - PERONNE road and fought a rearguard action to the FRAMERVILLE - VAUVILLERS line	

WAR DIARY or INTELLIGENCE SUMMARY

Army Form C. 2118.

Place	Date	Hour	Summary of Events and Information	Remarks and references to Appendices
AOXVILLERS	26/3/18		The Battalion held the line infront of VAUX VILLERS till the evening and was relieved by a composite Battalion under LIEUT COLONEL LITTLE DSO MC and took up a position in front of HARBONNIERES.	
CAYEUX	27/3/18		On the morning of the 27th did the enemy again attacked with the Battalion holding which was obliged in a counter attack. From there the Battalion withdrew to CAYEUX and again took up a position and was again forced to withdraw to the MARCELCAVE - INGACOURT line.	
AUBERCOURT	28/3/18		On the 28th the enemy attacked and pressed the Battalion to the AUBERCOURT where a stand was made in the evening and the enemy broken off. On the day the Battalion was in touch with the FRENCH on our right.	
	29/3/18		The Battalion withdrew to the DEMVIN lui after two days fighting and were withdrawn to WIETHANGARD here after a counter attack again.	
LONGEAU	3/3/18		On the 31st the Battalion was relieved by a a Battalion of the 1st Division and concentrated at LONGEAU. Early in the morning the Battalion marched to PISSY.	

WAR DIARY
or
INTELLIGENCE SUMMARY.

(Erase heading not required.)

Place	Date	Hour	Summary of Events and Information	Remarks and references to Appendices
	3/3/18		During the time from March 21st/31st the Battalion was continually in action and fought very hard. The casualties were 25 Officers and 630 ORs.	
			Honours + Character numerous as follows:-	
			AWARDED D.S.O. — LT. COL. E. E. KIPPAX M.C. 5.3.18	
			LIEUT. N. KENNEDY 21.3.18	
			2/LIEUT. G. HUNT M.C. 21.3.18	
			" H. HEATER 21.3.18	
			" A.C. MASON 23.3.18	
			LIEUT. A. GREEN 20.3.18	
			WOUNDED	
			LIEUT. COL. E. E. KIPPAX D.S.O. 22.3.18	
			MAJOR T. E. HOWORTH 23.3.18	
			CAPT. + ADJT. O.J. SITTON M.C. 22.3.18	
			CAPT. E. H. SCOTT 21.3.18	
			CAPT. A. R. MAK 21.3.18 (Gas)	
			LIEUT. F. HUTTON 21.3.18 (Gas)	
			LIEUT. A.S. JONES 21.3.18	
			LIEUT. G.F. TILL 21.3.18	
			LIEUT. H. KERSHAW 24.3.18	
			LIEUT. H. STONES M.C. 26.3.18	
			2/LIEUT. J.G. HINKS 27.3.18	
			2/LIEUT. A.J. BRADLEY 26.3.18	

INTELLIGENCE SUMMARY

(Erase heading not required.)

Place	Date	Hour	Summary of Events and Information	Remarks and references to Appendices
	2-3-17 (cont'd)		Casualties - Officers - Cont'd. WOUNDED (CONT'D) 2/LIEUT. H. HOLDSTOCK 24-3-18 2/LIEUT. M. WITTY 21-3-18 (GAS) 2/LIEUT. N.N. SHEPHARD 21-3-18 LIEUT. W.H. QUINNEY 24-3-18 MISSING CAPT. F. HOOD. M.C. 22-3-18 CAPT. J.E. BUTTERWORTH 24-3-18 2/LIEUT. M. POKMER 24-3-18	

D. Shielli
Comm Officer 9th Bn. Worcester Regt.

SECRET.   9th Battn. The Manchester Regiment.   Copy No. 15
                            ORDERS NO. 4.

Vol. II. APP. A.

In the Field,
7th March, 1918.

Ref. Map 62c 1/40,000
MARCOURT 1/10,000.

1.   The Battalion will relieve the 2/5th Bn. E. LANCS. RGT.
in the Front Line of the Centre Brigade, on the 8th March, 1918.

2.   Companies will relieve sister Companies of 2/5th Bn. E.
LANCS. RGT. and will be disposed as follows, Front Line, from
Right to Left, "A","B", "D" Coys. "C" Coy. will be in reserve.

3.   Order of relief— "A", "B", "C" Coys., Battn. H. Qrs., "D" Coy.

4. GUIDES.
        Guides for "A", "B", "C" Coys. and H.Qrs. will be at
Junction of road and light railway in L.10.a. at 2-30 p.m.
Guides for "D" Coy. will be at the same place at 3-30 p.m.
"D" Coy. will move up to L.10.a. and take over billets
vacated by "C" Coy., by 3-30 p.m.

5.   Trench Stores, Defence schemes and schemes of work will
be taken over and receipts sent to Battn. H.Qrs. within 4
hours of relief. Sketch Maps, showing dispositions, will
be sent to Battn. H.Qrs. as soon as possible after relief.
Completion of relief will be reported by wire (using the code
words A.B.(4.) and by runner.

6.   Blankets and Officers valises.   Blankets will be tied
in bundles of 10 and dumped ready for collection by T.O. by
9-0 a.m. Officers valises will be dumped at Bn. & Coy. H.Qrs.,
one hour before moving off, and will be collected by T.O.

7.   Rations for "A", "B", & "C" Coys. and H.Qrs. will be sent
to Junction of road and light railway at L.5.c.4.0. by 6-30 p.m.
"C" Coy. will provide ration party for "A" & "B" Coys. "D" Coy.
will provide its own ration party. Dixies will be taken to the
line.

8.   Water Arrangements.   Water for cooking is
obtained at the well at L.5.c.5.0.   Q.M. will arrange to send
up daily 8 petrol tins of water for drinking for each Coy. and
Battn. H.Qrs.

9. TRANSPORT.
                            Maltese Cart and Mess Cart
will report at 5-30 p.m. Field Cooker of "D" Coy. will be
taken to transport lines by T.O. during afternoon of 8th inst.
Field Cooker of "D" Coy. will remain in MESNECOURT for use of
details. No transport will be required for Lewis Guns.
G.S. Wagon will be provided for transport of blankets.

        O.C. "A" Coy. will leave behind surplus for whom there is
no accommodation in the Line. They will report to MAJOR
HAMILTON in MESNECOURT at 3-0 p.m. and will remain there under
his orders in billets vacated by detachment of 2/5th Bn. E.
LANCS. RGT. Details at present at the Transport Lines will
move under orders of Major HAMILTON.

        O.C. "C" Coy. will take over the Gum boot store and the
reserve rations and will check them carefully.

        O.C. Coys. will arrange for an Officer to hand over
billets and papers, etc., to relieving Coys.

acknowledge.

                                (sd) C. J. Sutton,
                                Captain & Adjutant,
                            9th Battn. The Manchester Regiment.

DISTRIBUTION:-

Copy   Nos. 1. 198 Infy. Bde.
            2. C.O.
         3/6 O.C. Coys.
         7/8 Q.M./T.O.
            9. Medical Officer.
           10. O.C. 4th Bn. E. LANCS. RGT.
           11. O.C. 2/5th Bn. E. LANCS. RGT.
           12. 2nd in Command.
           13. Lieut. Till.
           14. R.S.M.
       15/16. War Diary.
           17. File.
           18. Spare.

Issued by...Runner...... at....7.45 hrs.

Secret   VOL. II. APP. B.
                              G 5

O.C. Coys A
           B
           C
           D

1   The Battalion will be brought into a two Company front to-day.

2   O.C. A Coy will take over the area occupied by B Coy to the right of ONION LANE exclusive, as explained to Coy Commanders of A & B this morning. The relief to be completed this afternoon.

3   O.C. C Coy will relieve with one platoon the portion of B Coy from ONION LANE inclusive to the left of B Coy boundary. This will be done this afternoon in accordance with verbal instructions given by C.O. this morning.

4   On relief B Coy will be accommodated near The EGG and at BOBBY FARM and BOBBY QUARRY. Dispositions will be in accordance with attached sketch A (2nd in B Coy only)

5   Accommodation as laid down for this Coy is as follows. The second column shows accommodation at present available

		At present
RR EGG	2 Platoons.	30 OR now at EGG at 6.116-75.75
BOBBY QUARRY	Coy. Platoon H.Q. 1 Platoon	26 OR.
BOBBY FARM	1 Platoon	1 off 12 OR.

5. Unit accommodation is available at for Coy H.Q. at BOBBY QUARRY Coy H.Q. will be accommodated with C Coy H.Q. (D Coy when relieved) near Battn. H.Q.

1 Platoon will be accommodated at new R. EGG, one at BOBBY QUARRY and 1 at BOBBY FARM and in elephant shelter at present occupied by raiding party of D Coy. Coy cookhouse for B Coy will be retained by Pat Coy. The platoon at BOBBY QUARRY will probably require a separate cookhouse which will be found already constructed there.

O.J. Sutton
Capt. Adjt
KID

12.3.18
12.40 p

Vol. II. APP. C.
Copy No.

SECRET.
NHM UHHUM.

"K I D" Orders No.6.

In the Field,
15th March 1916.

REF. MAP, RANCICOURT Special Sheet 1/10,000.

The Battalion will be relieved by GRAIOIS to-morrow, 16th inst.

RELIEF.   Order of relief will be as follows:-
    "A" KID relieved by "B" GRAIOIS.
    "D" "   "   " "A"   "
    "B" "   "   " "C"   "
    "C" "   "   " "D"   "

GUIDES.   Guides from "A", "B" & "D" Coys. KID will report
to 2nd Lieut. WILLIS at junction of Cross Roads and Railway,
L.10.b.4.7. at 3-30 p.m. Guides from "D" Coy. will be at same
place at 6-0 p.m. Platoon Guides will be picked up at Coy. H.Qrs.

    On relief Coys. will move to HARVILLE. Movement E. of L.10...
will be in sections, West of that place by platoons, at 200 yards
distance. All Officers and N.C.Os. must be informed of their
Battle Stations beforehand in case of alarm.

    Trollies must be loaded by 2-30 p.m. and will be sent from
A. Qrs. by 3-0 p.m. to L.10...

    All disposition Maps, Defence and Work Schemes, and
Documents relating to the Sector will be handed over.
    All Trench stores, including anti-Gas appliances and Gas
curtains will be handed over carefully and copies of receipts, in
duplicate, sent to Battn. H.Qrs. soon after relief, and must tally,
so far as possible, with receipts given on taking over.
    Separate receipts will be obtained for Reserve Rations and
Water, and also for Boots in Gum Boot Stores.
    Besides the Petrol Tins for Reserve Water, 10 with "A" Coy.
are trench stores.
    Certificates of cleanliness must be forwarded by 9-0 a.m.
17th inst.

TRANSPORT.   Mess Cart and Maltese Cart will be at L.10.a. at
3-30 p.m.   L.G. Limbers of "A", "B", & "D" Coys. at 4-30 p.m.
Coys. must keep in touch with their L.G. Limbers on the way down.
1 extra Limber for dixies, etc., at 4-0 p.m.
Ride horses for "A", "B", & "D" Coys at 4-30 p.m., for O.C., Adjt.,
and M.O. at 9-0 p.m. at Well L.11.a.6.9.
L.G. Limbers and ride horse for "C" Coy. at "C" Coy. Cookhouse,
8-30 p.m.

    Q.M. and C.Q.M.Sgt. will take over billets at HARVILLE.
C.Q.M.Sgts. will guide their Coys. to the billets on arrival.
Q.M. will arrange for Baths.

    Attention is directed to Working Party Table, to be issued
lately.

    Details at RANCICOURT will move to HARVILLY under orders of
MAJOR HASALTON.

ACKNOWLEDGE.

Distribution - NORMAL.   (Sd.) C.J. Sutton,
                                 Captain & Adjutant,
                                        K.I.D.

Confidential.

WAR DIARY

INTELLIGENCE SUMMARY.

WAR DIARY

9TH. BATTALION

THE

MANCHESTER

REGIMENT.

---o-o-o---

VOL. III.
APRIL, 1918.

Army Form C. 2118.

WAR DIARY
or
INTELLIGENCE SUMMARY.
(Erase heading not required.)

Instructions regarding War Diaries and Intelligence Summaries are contained in F. S. Regs., Part II. and the Staff Manual respectively. Title pages will be prepared in manuscript.

Place	Date	Hour	Summary of Events and Information	Remarks and references to Appendices

A.5834. Wt. W4973/M687 750,000 8/16 D. D. & L. Ltd. Forms/C.2118/13.

Army Form C. 2118.

WAR DIARY
or
INTELLIGENCE SUMMARY.

(Erase heading not required.)

Instructions regarding War Diaries and Intelligence Summaries are contained in F. S. Regs. Part II. and the Staff Manual respectively. Title pages will be prepared in manuscript.

Place	Date	Hour	Summary of Events and Information	Remarks and references to Appendices
PISSY	April 1st. 1918.		The Battalion on being relieved from the line, concentrated at PISSY.	
	2nd.		The Battalion (less Transport) marched to SALEUX during the morning and entrained for LONGPRE. The Battalion arrived at LONGPRE about 2.30p.m. and marched to BISSUS-BUSSUEL, and was accommodated in Billets there. Transport moved by road from PISSY to BISSUS-BUSSUEL arriving about 8.30p.m.	
BISSUS-BUSSUEL	3rd.		Battalion was inspected by Brigadier-General HUNTER, M.C., Cmdg. 198th. Infantry Brigade.	
	4th.		The Battalion carried out training. Range firing practice was carried out during the morning.	
	5th.		Battalion moved by march route to HAUTVILLERS - DRUCAT Area, via ST. RIQUER. Major H.G. FRASER rejoined Battalion from Senior Officers' Course, ALDERSHOT. 2/Lieut. H. WILCOCK Rejoined Battalion from Leave to United Kingdom. For details of move see appendix "A".	Appendix "A"

9th Battalion Manchester Regt.

Army Form C. 2118.

WAR DIARY
or
INTELLIGENCE SUMMARY.

(Erase heading not required.)

Instructions regarding War Diaries and Intelligence Summaries are contained in F.S. Regs., Part II. and the Staff Manual respectively. Title pages will be prepared in manuscript.

Place	Date	Hour	Summary of Events and Information	Remarks and references to Appendices
HAUTVILLERS	April 6th.		Battalion was engaged in Training.	
	7th.			
	8th.		Battalion was engaged in Training.	
	9th.			
	10th			
	11th.			
COULON-VILLERS.	12th.		The Battalion (less Transport and Details) moved to COULONVILLERS; and formed a Company and Battalion Headquarters of the Manchester Composite Battalion, under Lieut-Colonel J.L. Heselton, D.S.O.,	
			For details of move see appendix "B".	Appendix "B".
			Transport and Details remained at HAUTVILLERS.	
LONG	13th.		The Manchester Composite Battalion moved to LONG, and were established in Billets there.	
			Transport and Details moved to MILLENCOURT.	
MILLENCOURT	14th.		Details of move see appendix "C".	Appendix "C"

[signature]
9th Battalion Manchester Regt.

A5834. Wt.W4973/M687 750,000 8/16 D.D.&L. Ltd. Forms/C.2118/13.

Army Form C. 2118.

WAR DIARY
or
INTELLIGENCE SUMMARY.
(Erase heading not required.)

Instructions regarding War Diaries and Intelligence Summaries are contained in F.S. Regs., Part II. and the Staff Manual respectively. Title pages will be prepared in manuscript.

Place	Date	Hour	Summary of Events and Information	Remarks and references to Appendices
LONG	14th. (Contd).		The Manchester Composite Battalion carried out training.	
MILLENCOURT	15th.		Battalion Headquarters joined Transport and details at Millencourt.	
			Battalion Training Cadre was formed under Lieut-Colonel J.L. HESELTON, D.S.O.,	
			For nominal roll of Cadre see appendix "D"	Appendix "D"
			The Manchester Composite Battalion remained at LONG and carried out extensive training.	
	16th.		Battalion Headquarters, Transport and Cadre remained at MILLENCOURT.	
			The Manchester Composite Battalion carried out training at LONG.	
LE PLESSIEL	17th.		Battalion Headquarters, Transport and Cadre Moved to LE PLESSIEL.	
			Remainder of Battalion remained at LONG at carried out instruction under the Composite Battalion.	

9th Battalion Manchester Regt.

Army Form C. 2118.

WAR DIARY
or
INTELLIGENCE SUMMARY.

(Erase heading not required)

Instructions regarding War Diaries and Intelligence Summaries are contained in F. S. Regs., Part II. and the Staff Manual respectively. Title pages will be prepared in manuscript.

Place	Date	Hour	Summary of Events and Information	Remarks and references to Appendices
LE PLESSIEL	18th.		Battalion Headquarters, Transport and Cadre remained at LE PLESSIEL and carried out Training	
	19th.			
	20th.			
	21st.		Battalion Headquarters, Cadre and Transport moved to SETQUES, entraining at LONGPRE. For details of move see appendix "E". The remainder of B attalion joined Battn. Headquarters. The composite Battalion was disbanded.	Appendix "E"
	22nd.			
	23rd.		The Battalion carried out training at SETQUES	
	24th.			

9th Battalion Manchester Regt.

Army Form C. 2118.

WAR DIARY
or
INTELLIGENCE SUMMARY.

(Erase heading not required.)

Instructions regarding War Diaries and Intelligence Summaries are contained in F. S. Regs., Part II. and the Staff Manual respectively. Title pages will be prepared in manuscript.

Place	Date	Hour	Summary of Events and Information	Remarks and references to Appendices
SETQUES	24th.		Immediate awards by the Commander-in-chief were published in Divisional Routine Orders.	
			For list of Officer and Other Rank recipients see appendix "F".	Appendix "F"
	25th.		2nd. Lieut. F. P. ELLIOTT and 289 Other Ranks were despatched to Base, being surplus under Training Cadre Scheme.	
			Major H.G. Fraser, proceeded to 25th. Division to assume appointment of 2nd-in-Command of a Battalion.	
BELLEBRUNE	26th.		Battalion Cadre and Transport moved by road to BELLEBRUNE, and were established in Billets there. Battalion Headquarters at the CHATEAU.	
	27th.		The Commanding Officer, Adjutant, and Signalling Officer, and 4 O.R's. proceeded to RYVELD, where they supervised CHINESE Labour in the construction of a new Line.	
	28th. 29th. 30th.		The Cadre carried out training at BELLEBRUNE.	
			The Cadre carried out training at BELLEBRUNE.	

9th Battalion Manchester Regt.

SECRET Copy No. 9

APPENDIX "A"

9TH. BATTALION THE MANCHESTER REGIMENT.

ORDER NO. 67

dated Friday April 5th. 1918.

Reference Sheets :- ABBEVILLE & LENS, 1/100,000

1. The Battalion will move to-day, April 5th. to HAUTVILLERS - DRUCAT Area.

2. THE Battalion will be drawn up outside the Battalion Headquarters, in the following order, at 8.0a.m.

    "A" Company,
    "B" Company,
    "C" Company,
    "D" Company,

3. Transport will be ready to move at 8.0a.m. and will proceed with Battalion.

4. Officers' Kits, Mess Kits, and Blankets (tied in bundles of ten), will be dumped at the Quartermaster's Store by 7.0a.m.

5. The strictest attention will be paid by Os. C. Companies to march discipline.

6. Route :- ST. RIQUIER.

(Signed) P. DARLINGTON,
2nd. Lieut.
Acting Adjutant,
9th. Battalion The Manchester Regiment.

Copies to :-

   No. 1. Commanding Officer
       2. O. C. "A" Company,
       3. O. C. "B" Company,
       4. O. C. "C" Company,
       5. O. C. "D" Company,
       6. The Transport Officer,
       7. The Quartermaster,
       8. The R. S. M.
       9. War Diary
      10. War Diary
      11. File.

SECRET   APPENDIX 'B'   Copy No. 12

9TH. BATTALION THE MANCHESTER REGIMENT.

O R D E R   N O.   8.

dated April 12th. 1918.

Reference Sheets, ABBEVILLE, 14. 1/100,000
                  LENS, II., 1/10 0,000.

1. The Battalion will move to COULONVILLERS Area to-day.

2. The Battalion will parade in front of Battalion Headquarters at 7. 30a.m.

3. Officer's Kits and Blankets in bundles of tens will be dumped in Battalion Headquarters, yard by 7. 0a.m. Quartermaster will arrange for loading above, to be complete by 7. 45a.m. These will accompany the Battalion.

4. Transport Officer will arrange for 4 Lewis Guns and full complement of S. A. A. and necessary Transport to be at Battalion Headquarters at 7. 45a.m.

5. Rations for the 13th. inst. will be issued and will be carried by the men.

6. Transport and Quartermaster's Stores, with the exception of that detailed above will remain in present area.

7. The undermentioned will not accompany Battalion:-

        Transport Staff
        Quartermaster's Staff
        Demonstration Platoon
        Divisional Guard
        C.Q.M.S's.
        Water Duty Men
        Bn. Postman
        Orderly Room Staff
        351206 Sgt. Allen, G.
        1 Cook per Company.

8. Coys will march in 30/

9. D. Coys Mess Box will be taken with Officers Kits

(Signed) P. DARLINGTON,
2/Lieut.,
Acting Adjutant,
9th. Battalion The Manchester Regiment.

Distribution :-
    Copy No. 1.   198th. Infantry Brigade.
            2   Commanding Officer
            3   O. C. "A" Company,
            4   O. C. "B" Company,
            5   O. C. "C" Company,
            6   O. C. "D" Company,
            7   The Medical Officer
            8   The Transport Officer
            9   The Quartermaster
      10. & 11   War Diary
           12   File

SECRET

APPENDIX 'C'   Copy No. 10

9TH. BATTALION THE MANCHESTER REGIMENT

DETAILS

ORDER No. I

Dated April 13th. 1918.

Reference Sheet, ABBEVILLE, 14, 1/100,000.

1. Details will move to MILLENCOURT Area to-day.

2. Details will parade at 10.45a.m. outside Battalion Headquarters.

3. DRESS :- Full Marching Order, Steel Helmets will be worn.

4. Blankets tied in bundles of ten and Officer's Kits will be handed in to the Quartermaster's Stores by 9.0a.m.

5. C.Q.M.S's. of "A" and "B" Companies will proceed to MILLENCOURT as billeting party to be there by 10.0a.m.

6. Transport will move with details.

7. Billets must be left in a clean and sanitary condition.

8. Details will march in 3's

9. Surplus Transport personnel will march with details

(Signed) P. DARLINGTON,
2/Lieut.,
Acting Adjutant,
9th. Battn. The Manchester Regiment.

Distribution :-
   Copy No. 1 :- The Commanding Officer,
       2 :- Major C. E. Welch,
       3 :- The Transport Officer,
       4 :- C.Q.M.S. "A" Company,
       5 :- C.Q.M.S. "B" Company,
       6 :- C.Q.M.S. "C" Company,
       7 :- C.Q.M.S. "D" Company,
       8 :- i/c Quartermaster Stores.
       9 :- File.
      10 :- War Diary

Appendix 'D'

9TH. BATTALION THE MANCHESTER REGIMENT.

TRAINING CADRE

Commanding Officer	Lieut-Colonel, J.L. Heselton, D.S.O., M.C.,
Adjutant	2/Lieut. B. DARLINGTON, M.C.,
Hon. Lieut. & Quartermaster	Lieut. W. Tarpey,
Lewis Gun Officer	2/Lieut. A. G. Shillinglaw,
Scout Officer	2/Lieut. H. J. Chapman,
Signalling Officer	2/Lieut. A.E. Hedges, M.C.,

'D'

Battalion Cadre (Continued).

R.S.M.	350074	C.S.M.	Grantham, H. D.C.M.,
R.Q.M.S.	350856	R.Q.M.S.	Marshall, A.
Q.M. Staff	45301	Pte.	Goffett, V.
	350738	"	Smith, T.
	352113	"	Garratt, W.
Orderly Room Clerk	352957	Sergt.	Wilson, J.
Police	352414	Corpl.	Bottrell, H.

Sergeant Instructors

Musketry	351914	Sergt.	Fairbrother, R.
	351208	"	Allen, G.
	200969	Cpl.	Smalley, W.
	350680	"	Chadderton, H.
	51432	"	Hewson, T.
P.T. & B.F.	350714	Sergt.	Moss, J., D.C.M.,
Lewis Gun	352566	Sergt.	Hilditch, H.
	351724		Collins, H.
Rifle Bombing	201445	Corpl.	McTighe, W.
Gas Personnel	350218	"	Matley, E.C.
Cook	350642	L/Cpl.	Haigh, F.
Batmen	373001	Pte.	Bennett, J.S.
	44802	"	Biss, A.W.
	352079	"	Graham, E.J.
	350278	"	Smith, H.
	350724	"	Hall, H.
	5956	"	Holt, J.
	351483	"	Reece, C.
	49315	"	Hatfield, H.
	350282	"	Winterbottom, A.
	350450	"	Gaskell, W.
	37151	"	Baxendale, H.
	353050	L/Cpl.	Fairhurst, J.
	10141	Pte.	Hart, W.
Transport	352163	Pte.	Rushton, J.
	351830	"	Hudson, J.
Grooms	351336	L/Cpl.	Spiby, H.
	350995	Pte.	Chadwick, G.Y.
Water Duty	401172	Pte.	Braddock, T.
Sanitary Duties	350775	L/Sergt.	Harding, R.
Postman	350894	L/Cpl.	Harrison, E.
Additional Instructors	352868	Sergt.	Outram, J.
	350312	Corpl.	Sayle, T.

'D'

"A" Company

Company Commander		2/Lieut. O. Hamilton,	
C. S. M.	351033	C. S. M.	Travis, R.
C.Q.M.S.	14128	C.Q.M.S.	Whitehead, H. M.M.
Gas Personnel	351014	Corpl. Pte.	Morris,
Lewis Gun Instructor	351327	Pte.	Holt, H.

"B" Company

Company Commander		Lieut. A. J. Statham,	
C. S. M.	351419	C. S. M.	Lawler, H.
C.Q.M.S.	351036	C.Q.M.S.	Calvert, W.
Gas Personnel	350459	Corpl.	Gorman, F.
Lewis Gun Instructor	201970	Pte.	Strettle, E.

"C" Company

Company Commander		2/Lieut. E. Potter	
C. S. M.	351008	C. S. M.	Ashton, J.
C.Q.M.S.	351384	C.Q.M.S.	Mason, W.H.
Gas Personnel	352863	Corpl.	Hewitt, C.
Lewis Gun Instructor	353454	Pte.	Mason, J.

"D" Company

Company Commander		2/Lieut. H. Wilcock,	
C. S. M.	350705	C. S. M.	Martin, W.
C.Q.M.S.	351384	C.Q.M.S.	Tetlow, Z.
Gas Personnel	44742	Corpl.	Gunn, A.E.
Lewis Gun Instructor	54415	Pte.	Pratt, W.

ATTACHED

Capt. H. Smith, R. C. Chaplain.

2428 S/Sergt. Thompson, A.T.

APPENDIX 'E'   Copy No. ......11......

9th. BATTALION THE MANCHESTER REGIMENT.

ORDER NO. 74.

Dated April 21st. 1918.

1. The Battalion will entrain at LONGPRE on the 22nd. inst.

2. PARADE. The Battalion will parade at 1145p.m. in front of Battalion Headquarters.

3. DRESS. Marching Order less pack. Ground sheets rolled on the belt. Steel Helmets will be worn.

   Packs marked with the owner's name will be handed in to the Quartermaster's Stores by 6. 0p.m. to-day.

4. RATIONS. Rations for consumption on the 22nd. will be drawn and carried by each man. Quartermaster will arrange for cooking and distribution of any uncooked rations.
   Every man will march away with his water bottle filled.

5. TRANSPORT. Transport less Officers' Kit wagon will be packed before 6. 0p.m. to-night.
   Transport will be ready to move off at 11. 30p.m. and 2/Lieut. A. G. SHILLINGLAW, will report arrival of Transport to Divisional Representative at LONGPRE at 6. 0a.m.

6. BREAKFASTS. Quartermaster will arrange for breakfasts for the Battalion at 11. 0p.m. to-night.

7. DISCIPLINE. The Battalion will march in 3's and strict march discipline will be enforced.

8. MOUNTS. Following Mounts will not move with Transport but with the Battalion :-
   Commanding Officer's
   Second-in-Command's
   Adjutant's
   Medical Officer's
   Quartermaster's
   I Company Mount (Jack).

9. MESS KITS, ETC., Mess Kits and Officer's Valises will be handed in to Quartermaster and packed by 9. 0p.m.

10. ARRIVAL. Transport Officer will arrange for Transport Cooks to prepare tea for men on arrival at LONGPRE.

11. OFFICE. This Office will close at 9. 0p.m.

(Signed) P. DARLINGTON,
2/Lieut.,
Acting Adjutant,
9th. Battalion The Manchester Regt.

Distribution :-
- Copy No. 1. Commanding Officer   No. 6 2/Lt. H. Wilcock,
       2   Second-in-Command   7 "   H.J. Chapman,
       3   2/Lt. A.G. Shillinglaw   8 Quartermaster
       4   "   A. V. Hedges   9 R. S. M.
       5   "   E. Porter   10 File.
                                     11 War Diary

APPENDIX 'F'

9TH. BATTALION THE MANCHESTER REGIMENT.

HONOURS AND AWARDS FOR GALLANTRY DURING THE PERIOD
MARCH 21st. - 31st. 1918.

Bar to The Distinguished Service Order

    Lieut - Colonel E. C. LLOYD, D. S. O.,

Bar to The Military Cross

    Capt. W. BROWNE BAGSHAW, M.C.,

THE Military Cross

    Lieut - Colonel J. L. HESELTON, D. S. O.,
    2/Lieut. A. T. HEDGES,
    2/Lieut. A. J. BRADLEY,

Distinguished Conduct Medal

    350714 Sergt. J. Moss,

Military Medal

14178	C.Q.M.S.	Whitehead,	H.
352346	Sergt.	Blunt,	J.
376173	Pte.	Hilditch,	W.
350776	"	Taylor,	W.
22457	"	Flaherty,	W.
352961	"	Sanderson,	S.

        The Commanding Officer heartily
congratulates the recipients.

CONFIDENTIAL.

WAR DIARY
OF
9TH BATTN: THE MANCHESTER REGIMENT

FROM MAY 1ST. TO MAY 31ST.
1918

VOLUME IV.

Army Form C. 2118.

WAR DIARY
or
INTELLIGENCE SUMMARY.
(Erase heading not required.)

Place	Date	Hour	Summary of Events and Information	Remarks and references to Appendices
BELLE BRUNE	MAY 1st		Battalion Cadre carried out training. Commanding Officer, Adjutant, Signalling Officer & O.R's returned from temporary attachment to 40th Bn.	
	2nd		Cadre (less Transport) proceeded to BRUTELLES, entraining at DESVRES, & detraining at NOYELLES. For details of move see Appendix "A". Transport remained at BELLE BRUNE under Lieut J HOLLINGSWORTH, M.M., awaiting disposal under Army arrangements.	Appendix "A"
BRUTELLES	3rd		Cadre was billeted in BRUTELLES arriving about noon.	

Army Form C. 2118

WAR DIARY
or
INTELLIGENCE SUMMARY.

(Erase heading not required.)

Summary of Events and Information

WAR DIARY
OF
9TH ATTACHED THE
MANCHESTER
REGIMENT

FROM 1ST JANUARY
1918
TO 11 OCTOBER

Place	Date	Hour		Remarks and references to Appendices

WAR DIARY
or
INTELLIGENCE SUMMARY

Army Form C. 2118.

Place	Date	Hour	Summary of Events and Information	Remarks and references to Appendices
BELLBRUNE	MAY 1st		Battalion bare carried out training. Commanding Officer Adjutant Signalling Officer + 4 O.R's returned from temporary attachment to 40th Div.	Appendix "A"
	2nd		Cadre (less transport) proceeded to BRUTELLES, entraining at DESVRES, & detraining at NOYELLES. For details of move see appendix "A". Transport remained at BELLEBRUNE under Lieut J HOLLINGSWORTH, M.M., awaiting dispersal under Army arrangements.	
BRUTELLES	3rd		Cadre was billeted at BRUTELLES arriving about noon.	

Army Form C. 2118.

WAR DIARY
or
INTELLIGENCE SUMMARY.
(Erase heading not required.)

Place	Date	Hour	Summary of Events and Information	Remarks and references to Appendices
BRUTELLES	MAY 4th		Cadre carried out training.	
	5th		Cadre carried out training in accordance with Battalion Orders	Appendix "G"
	6th		Topics of Battalion Orders see Appendix	
		12/147	R.S.M. TEMPLE (East Yorks. Regt.) reported for duty	
	7th		Cadre carried out training	
	8th			
	9th		Cadre carried out training	
			Capt. R.A KING, reported for duty.	

Army Form C. 2118.

WAR DIARY
or
INTELLIGENCE SUMMARY.
(Erase heading not required.)

Instructions regarding War Diaries and Intelligence Summaries are contained in F. S. Regs., Part II. and the Staff Manual respectively. Title pages will be prepared in manuscript.

Place	Date	Hour	Summary of Events and Information	Remarks and references to Appendices
BRUXELLES	MAY 10th		Cadre moved by march route to FRANLEU via ST BELMONT and then bivouacked in billets there at 1.30pm. Headquarters at to PETIT CHATEAU	APPENDIX "B"
FRANLEU	11th		A detail of men re Appendix B	
	12th		Cadre carried out training	
	13th		"G" Company 2nd Battalion 327th Regiment arrived at EU France were sent to connect 5 Company to FRANLEU where they arrived at 4.30 pm	
	14th		"E" Company 2nd Batt. 327th Regiment American Army arrived at CAMPAGNE about 2.30 pm "F" Company 2nd Bn. 327th Regiment American Army arrived at FRIRUELLES about 2.30 pm	

Army Form C. 2118.

WAR DIARY
or
INTELLIGENCE SUMMARY.
(Erase heading not required.)

Instructions regarding War Diaries and Intelligence
Summaries are contained in F.S. Regs., Part II.
and the Staff Manual respectively. Title pages
will be prepared in manuscript.

Place	Date	Hour	Summary of Events and Information	Remarks and references to Appendices
FRANLEU	MAY 15th		Carried out Training	
			'E' Company 2nd Bn. 327th Regt. moved to FRANLEU	
	16th		2/Lieut. P. DARLINGTON. M.C. appointed A/Adjutant and Adjutant with effect from 23/3/18.	APPENDIX "G" 18.5.18
	17th 18th 19th		Carried reported to their respective American Companies in accordance with Battalion Orders (see Appendix) dated 18.5.18. and assisted in Training of the American Troops.	
	20th		2/Lieut. D.T. CHAPMAN. 2/Lieut. E. PORTER. M.M. and 24 Other Ranks surplus to establishment, were despatched to BRAY. Instructional training of American troops was carried in accordance with training programme (see appendices "C" & "D".	APPENDICES "C" & "D"

WAR DIARY or INTELLIGENCE SUMMARY

Place	Date	Hour	Summary of Events and Information	Remarks and references to Appendices
FRANLEU	MAY 20th		2/Lieut A V HEDGES M.C. reported to 103rd Inf. Bde to take command from Signal Section during temporary absence of B. Sig. Officer.	
	21st 22nd 23rd 24th		Instructional training & demonstration Staff & Training of 2nd Batn. 327th Regiment American Army was carried out in accordance with training Programme. (Appendix "C" & "D")	
	25th		Batn. moved to MONTIERES (Rd. Metz DIEPPE 16. M110000) & were billeted there. See Appendix E	Appendix E
MONTIERES	26th		Details of move see Appendix E. "A" Company Coln. moved to TILLOY to be attached to 2nd Battn. 328th Regiment. "B" Company Coln. moved to HELICOURT to attached to 2nd Battn. 328th Regt. and instruct	

Army Form C. 2118.

WAR DIARY
or
INTELLIGENCE SUMMARY.
(Erase heading not required.)

Place	Date	Hour	Summary of Events and Information	Remarks and references to Appendices
MONTIERES	MAY 26th		Headquarters "C" and "D" Company Canes remained at MONTIERES to be attached to and instruct 1st & 2nd 328th Regiment.	
	27th		Tanks reported to their respective attached American Unit & carried out intensive training.	
	28th		Tanks moved to LAMBERCOURT (Ref. sheet ABBEVILLE 1/100,000) Headquarters "B" & "C" Companies remaining there. Watch of move see Appendix F. "A" Company Tanks moved to FRIBUELLES. "D" Company Tanks moved to FRANLEU.	Appendix F
	29th		Headquarters Canes moved to FRANLEU. "A" & "D" Company Tanks reported to and engaged in the instruction of 2nd Battalion 327th Regt.	

Army Form C. 2118.

WAR DIARY
or
INTELLIGENCE SUMMARY.

(Erase heading not required.)

Instructions regarding War Diaries and Intelligence Summaries are contained in F. S. Regs., Part II. and the Staff Manual respectively. Title pages will be prepared in manuscript.

Place	Date	Hour	Summary of Events and Information	Remarks and references to Appendices
FRANLEU	MAY 9/14		"B" and "D" Companies remained at LAMBERCOURT and reported to 3rd Battalion 327th Regiment & went in training	
	30th			
	31st		Forces reported to their respective specialist Units & assisted with training	

SECRET   Appendix "A"   Copy No. 10

9TH. BATTALION THE MANCHESTER REGIMENT.

ORDER NO. 79

dated May 2nd. 1918.

Reference Sheets,   CALAIS 13, 1/100000
                       ABBEVILLE, 14, 1/100,000.

Area.   1. The Battalion Cadre will move to-day to ST. VALERY-sur-SOMME.
Entraining Station DESVRES. Time of journey 4½ hours.

Parade.   2. Battalion Cadre will parade at 4.30p.m. to-day 2nd. May, in front of Battalion Orderly Room.

Dress.   3. Full marching Order. Steel helmets strapped on back of pack.

Blankets & Officers Valises.   4. Blankets in bundles of ten and Officers' Valises to be dumped at the Quartermaster's Stores by 12. Onoon.

Mess Kits.   5. Mess Kits to be handed in to Quartermaster's Stores by 2. 0p.m.

Transport   6. Cadre Transport will assemble at Battalion Orderly Room at 4. 0p.m. and proceed to DESVRES.
R. Q. M. S. Marshall will be in charge of this transport and will report arrival to 66th. Division Entraining Officer.

Surplus Transport will remain in present area under Sergeant Hollingworth who will act on detailed instructions issued.

Billeting Party.   7. Lieut. A. J. Statham and 3 Other Ranks will travel by train leaving DESVRES at 12. 50p.m. May 2nd., reporting to entraining Officer ½ hour before the train is timed to start.
On arrival at NOYELLES the party will report to the Staff Captain, 197th. Infantry Brigade for instructions regarding billets.

Discipline   8. Cadre will march in 3's. Mess tins, etc. must be carried in the pack.

(Signed) P. DARLINGTON,
2/Lieut.,
Acting Adjutant,
9th. Battalion The Manchester Regiment.

Distribution :-
Copy No. 1   Commanding Officer
         2   O. C. "A" Company,
         3   O. C. "B" Company,
         4   O. C. "C" Company,
         5   O. C. "D" Company,
         6   Transport Sergeant,
         7   Quartermaster.
         8   C. S. M. Lawler, H.
         9   File.
        10   War Diary

SECRET   Appendix "B"   Copy No. 11

9TH. BATTALION THE MANCHESTER REGIMENT

ORDER NO. 12

dated 10th. May, 1918.

Reference Sheet, ABBEVILLE, 14, 1/100,000

Move	The Battalion Cadre will move to FRANLEU to-day the 10th. May.
Parade	The Battalion will parade outside Battalion Orderly Room at 9. 30a.m.
Dress	Full marching Order. Helmets to be strapped on the back of the pack.
Blankets	Blankets will be rolled in bundles of ten and handed in to the Quartermaster's Stores by 7. 0a.m.
Valises Mess Kits	Officers' Valises, and Mess Kits to be handed in to the Quartermaster's Stores by 7. 0a.m.
Discipline	The Battalion will march in column of threes.
Billeting	Lieut. A. J. STATHAM will proceed to FRANLEU to arrange billets.

(Signed) P. DARLINGTON,
2/Lieut.,
Acting Adjutant,
9th. Battalion The Manchester Regiment.

Distribution :-
Copy No. 1   The Commanding Officer
        2   O. C. "A" Company,
        3   O. C. "B" Company
        4   O. C. "C" Company,
        5   O. C. "D" Company,
        6   The Signalling Officer
        7   The Lewis Gun Officer
        8   Quartermaster
        9   The R.S.M.
     10   War Diary
     11   War Diary
     12   File
     13   Spare.

SECRET

APPENDIX "C"

PROGRAMME OF TRAINING. MAY 20th - 26th.

	8 - 8.30	8.30 - 9.0	9.0 - 9.30	9.30 - 10.30	10.30 - 11.0	11.0 - 11.30	11.30 - 12.0	2.0 - 4.0	REMARKS
MONDAY	PHYSICAL DRILL	BAYONET FIGHTING	GAS DRILL	MUSKETRY	BOMBING & RIFLE FROM HIP	PLATOON DRILL	GAS	FIRING ON 30" RANGE	(A) MUSKETRY INCLUDES LECTURES ON CARE OF ARMS, RAPID LOADING, SIGHTING & TRIGGER PRESSING, KNEELING, PROME AND STANDING POSITIONS. AIMING AND RAPID FIRE, JUDGING DISTANCE
TUESDAY	PHYSICAL DRILL	BAYONET FIGHTING	GAS DRILL	MUSKETRY	BOMBING & RIFLE BOMBING	PLATOON DRILL	GAS	FIRING ON 30" RANGE	(B) CLOSE ORDER DRILL OVER SCHOOL OF THE PLATOON EACH DAY
WEDNESDAY	PHYSICAL DRILL	BAYONET FIGHTING	GAS DRILL	MUSKETRY	BOMBING & RIFLE BOMBING	OPEN ORDER RAPID EXTENSIONS	GAS	FIRING ON 30" RANGE	(C) EACH DAY CLASSES WILL BE PARADED & GROUPING OVER FORMED BY O.C.
THURSDAY	PHYSICAL DRILL	BAYONET FIGHTING	GAS DRILL	MUSKETRY	BOMBING & RIFLE BOMB M.G.	OPEN ORDER RAPID EXTENSIONS	GAS	FIRING ON 30" RANGE	(D) LECTURES ON MUSKETRY, COMPASS, RECONNAISSANCE TO BE ARRANGED BY BATTALION OFFICER DETAILED.
FRIDAY	PHYSICAL DRILL	BAYONET FIGHTING	GAS DRILL	FIRE DIRECTION FIRE CONTROL USE OF COVER RECOGNITION OF TARGETS	BOMBING & RIFLE BOMBING	DRILL	GAS	FIRED ON 30" RANGE	(E) BOMBING INCLUDES THROWING, TYPES OF BOMBS
SATURDAY	PHYSICAL DRILL	BAYONET FIGHTING	GAS 11-12.15	(PLATOONS) INSTRUCTION IN KINDS OF WEAPONS	BOMBING & RIFLE BOMBING	LUNATRY DRILL	GAMES, CROSS COUNTRY RUNNING	SPORTS	(G) GAS INCLUDES MUSKETRY WHILE WEARING HELMETS, USES OF GAS

Appendix "D"

PROGRAMME OF TRAINING
LEWIS GUN.

Day	1st. Hour	2nd. Hour	3rd. Hour	4th. Hour	5th. Hour
Monday	Description	Description	Stripping	Mechanism	Care and Cleaning
Tuesday	Description	Stripping	Mechanism	Mechanism	Points before, during & after firing
Wednesday	Mechanism	Magazine Filling	Stoppage No. 1	Stripping	Examination and repairs
Thursday	Stripping	Gun Drill	Mechanism	Stoppage No. 1	Description (Pupils).
Friday	Mechanism	Stoppage No. 2	Gun Drill	Firing positions Fire orders	Aiming Drill Fire Orders
Saturday	Mechanism (Pupils)	Stoppage No. 2	Stoppages No. 1 & 2	Gun Drill	Care and Cleaning
Monday	Description	Mechanism	Mechanism	Gun Drill	Points before, during & after firing
Tuesday	Organization of Sections	Stoppage No. 3	Mechanism	Judging Distances	Fire Orders
Wednesday	Practical use of Ground	Elementary Tactics	Stoppages 1, 2, & 3	Mechanism	Fire Orders
Thursday	Range Work	Range Work	Range Work	Care and Cleaning	Care and Cleaning
Friday	Description	Stripping	Stoppages	Mechanism	Duties of No. 1 & 2
Saturday	Examination				

"E" Appendix "E"

SECRET   Copy No. 10

9TH. BATTALION THE MANCHESTER REGIMENT

ORDER NO. 13

dated May 25th. 1918

Reference Sheets, ABBEVILLE 14, 1/100,000
                   DIEPPE   16, 1/100,000

Move	Cadre will move to MONTIERES to-day 25th. May.
Parade	Cadre will parade at 11.30a.m. in front of Cadre Billet. "A" Company will join Cadre at CHEPY at 12.30p.m.
Dress	Full marching order, steel helmets strapped on the back of the pack.
Blankets	Blankets will be rolled in bundles of ten and handed in to Quartermaster's Store by 9.0a.m.
Officers' Kit - Mess Kit.	Officers' Kit and Mess Kit will be handed in to Quartermaster's Store by 9.30a.m.
Discipline	Billets will be left clean and all sanitary precautions taken.

(Signed) P. DARLINGTON,
Captain,
Adjutant,
9th. Battalion The Manchester Regt.

Distribution :-

    1   O. C. 2nd. Batsn. 327th. Regt.
    2   Commanding Officer
    3   O. C. "A" Company,
    4   O. C. "B" Company,
    5   O. C. "C" Company,
    6   O. C. "D" Company,
    7   The Quartermaster,
    8   The Lewis Gun Officer.
    9   The R. S. M.
   10   War Diary
   11   War Diary
   12   File.

SECRET   Copy No. 11

9TH. BATTALION THE MANCHESTER REGT.

ORDER NO. 14

Battalion Orders No. 28 is cancelled.

Reveille	Reveille at 5.15a.m.
Breakfast	Breakfast at 5.30a.m.
Move	Battalion Cadre will relieve the 4th. East Lancs. Regt. in MIANNEY Area to-morrow, 28th. inst.
Route	GAMACHES - HELICOURT - MASINIERES.
Parade	Parade at 7.0a.m. Dress :- Full marching order, Steel helmets strapped on back of pack.
Blankets	Blankets rolled in bundles of ten will be handed in to Quartermaster's Store by 6.0a.m.
Officers' Kits	Officers' Kits will be handed in to Quartermaster's Store by 6.0a.m.
Detached Company Cadres	Capt. R. H. KING and "A" Company Cadre will meet Battalion at Cross Roads 50 yards W of H in HELICOURT at 8.0a.m. Lieut. A. J. STATHAM and "B" Company Cadre will meet Battalion at cross roads 50 yards W of H in HELICOURT at 8.0a.m. O. C. "A" and "B" Companies will arrange for transportation of Kit and men's blankets to point of assembly.
Billeting Party	Quartermaster will proceed to MIANNEY and report to Officer Commanding 4th. East Lancs. Regt. at 10.0a.m.

2/Lieut. A. G. Shillinglaw will remain in this Area to hand over to representative of 4th. East Lancs. Regt.

(Signed) P. DARLINGTON,
Captain,
Adjutant,
9th. Battalion The Manchester Regiment.

Distribution :-
1. Commanding Officer
2. O. C. "A" Company,
3. O. C. "B" Company,
4. O. C. "C" Company,
5. O. C. "D" Company,
6. The Lewis Gun Officer
7. The Quartermaster,
8. R. S. M.
9. R. Q. M. S.
10. War Diary
11. War Diary
12. File.
13. Spare.

APPENDIX G

BATTALION ORDERS No. 5
BY
LIEUT-COLONEL J. L. HESELTON? D.S.O., M.C., Sunday,
CMDG. 9TH. BATTALION THE MANCHESTER REGIMENT.
5. 5. 18

Orderly Officer :-
   2/Lieut. H. J. Chapman.

1. **REVEILLE**
    Reveille at 6. 30a.m.
2. **BREAKFASTS**
    Breakfasts at 7. 30a.m.
3. **PARADES**
    Parade at 8. 55a.m.

9. 0a.m.	Inspection
9. 30a.m. - 11o 0a.m.	Arms Drill. Saluting Drill.
9. 30a.m. - 12. 45a.m.	Sergeant Collins will take the 4 men mentioned in para. 4 in Lewis Gun Training.

    Services
    R. C's. There will be a service in the Church, BRUTELLES. R.C's wishing to attend are excused the 9. 0a.m. parade.
    C. of E's.
    A service will be held at 12. 0noon at the HOTEL de la PLACE, BRUTELLES. Holy Communion after service.

4. **POSTINGS**
    The undermenioned men who joined the Unit to-day are posted to Companies as shown :-
      351327 Pte. Holt H. "A" Company
      201970 " Strettle, E. "B" Company
      353454 " Mason, J. "C" Company
      54415 " Pratt, W. "D" Company
    These men are for training as deputy Lewis Gun instructors.

5. **EXTRACTS**
    Attention of the Quartermaster is directed to G.R.O's 3899, 3900, 3903, 3909, and A. R. O's. 1996 and 1997.

6. **PROMOTIONS**
    Reference list of promotions attached.
    Company Commanders will arrange for A.Bs. 64 of N.C.Os concerned to be amended.

                                         P Darlington 2/Lieut.,
                                             Acting Adjutant,
                               9th. Battalion The Manchester Regt.

APPENDIX G.

BATTALION ORDERS
BY
LIEUT-COLONEL J. L. HESELTON, D.S.O., M.C.
CMDG. 9TH. BATTALION THE MANCHESTER REGIMENT.

No. 6
Monday
6. 5. 18

Orderly Officer :-
2/Lieut. A. V. Heiges, M.C.,

---

1. REVEILLE
   Reveille at 6. 30a.m.
2. BREAKFASTS
   Breakfasts at 7. 30a.m.
3. PARADES
   Parade at 8. 55a.m.

9. 0a.m. - 9. 30a.m.	Inspection
9. 30a.m. - 10. 0a.m.	Arms Drill.
10. 0am - 10. 30	P.T. & B.F. *Officers to take part*
10. 30a.m. - 11. 0a.m.	Saluting Drill
11. 0a.m. - 12. 30p.m.	Specialists training by sections.
9. 0a.m. - 12. 30p.m.	Sergeant Collins will instruct the 4 deputy Lewis Gunners in the Lewis Gun.

4. HAIRCUTTING   from 1 - 6 p.m.
   Pte. A. Winterbottom will be struck off all duties/ each Wednesday, and will be available at that time for the cutting of hair.
5. ORDERLY SERGEANT
   The R.S.M. will detail 1 Senior Sergeant and 1 Junior Sergeant to act as Cadre Orderly Sergeant and Supernumery Sergeant for the period of 3 days. The Orderly Sergeant will report to Battalion Orderly Room at 6. 30p.m. daily for detail and Battalion Orders for distribution to Company Commanders, etc.
6. BILLETS
   Attention will be paid by all ranks to the laying out of Kits and Blankets in accordance with the special way laid down as Regimental pattern.
7. ORDERLY OFFICER
   The Battalion Orderly Officer will inspect Billets before morning parade.

(Signed) P. DARLINGTON,
2/Lieut.,
Acting Adjutant,
9th. Battalion The Manchester Regiment.

Appendix G

BATTALION ORDERS No 9
BY
LIEUT-COLONEL J. L. HESELTON, D.S.O., M.C.   THURSDAY
COMMANDING 9TH. BATTALION THE MANCHESTER REGIMENT.
9. 5. 18.

Orderly Officer :-

2/Lieut. A. V. Hedges, M.C.

---

1. REVEILLE
    Reveille at 6.30 a.m.
2. BREAKFASTS
    Breakfasts at 7.30 a.m.
3. PARADES
    Parade at 8.55 a.m. Fall in at 9.0 a.m.

9. 0 a.m.	–	9. 30 a.m.	Inspection
9. 30 a.m.	–	10. 30 a.m.	Physical Training and Bayonet Fighting.
10. 45 a.m.	–	11. 15 a.m.	Communication Drill
11. 15 a.m.	–	12. Onoon	Musketry and Bolt Drill.
12. Onoon	–	12. 30 p.m.	Gas Drill and Training.
2. 0 p.m.	–	3. 30 p.m.	Lewis Gun Training.

(Signed) P. DARLINGTON,
2/Lieut.,
Acting Adjutant,
9th. Battalion The Manchester Regiment.

APPENDIX G

BATTALION ORDERS
BY
LIEUT-COLONEL J. L. HESELTON, D.S.O., M.C.
COMMANDING 9TH. BATTALION THE MANCHESTER REGIMENT.

No. 12
Sunday
12. 5. 18

Orderly Officer :-

2/Lieut. A. V. Hedges, M.C.

1. **REVEILLE**
   Reveille at 6.30a.m.
2. **BREAKFASTS**
   Breakfasts at 7.30a.m.
3. **PARADES**
   Parade in front of Billet at 9.0a.m. for inspection.
   Dress :- Belt and Bayonet.
   Orderly Officer will take this Parade.
   CHURCH PARADES
   R. C's will parade for Service in the Church, FRANLEU at 10.0a.m.
   Non-Conformists will parade for Service on Cadre Parade Ground at 10.45a.m.
4. **DISCIPLINE**
   The practice of shortening trousers or tightening them below the knee for wear with puttees will cease forthwith.
   Disciplinary action will be taken in the case of any infringement of this order, and in all cases those concerned will be charged with the trousers.
5. **SICK**
   W. Os. N.C.Os. and Men requiring Medical attendance will report sick to the Cadre Orderly Sergeant who will inform Battalion Orderly Room of names and billet of sick men before 9.0a.m.
6. **PARADE**
   All Officers excluding The Padre will attend Lecture by D.G.O. at BRUEULLES to-morrow at 11.0a.m.
   Location of Lecture Room to be notified later.
   All Officers to be seated by 10.55a.m.

(Signed) P. DARLINGTON,
2/Lieut.,
Acting Adjutant,
9th. Battalion The Manchester Regiment.

Appendix 'G'

BATTALION ORDERS No. 15
BY
LIEUT-COLONEL J. L. HESELTON, D.S.O., M.C.   Monday
COMMANDING 9TH. BATTALION THE MANCHESTER REGIMENT.
13. 5. 18

Orderly Officer :-

   2/Lieut. A. V. HEDGES, M. C.,

1. **REVEILLE**
    Reveille at 6. 30a.m.
2. **BREAKFASTS**
    Breakfasts at 7. 30 a.m.
3. **PARADES**
    Parade at 8. 55a.m.   Fall in at 9. 0a.m.

9. 0a.m. -	9. 15a.m.	Inspection
9. 30a.m. -	10. 30a.m.	Physical Training and Bayonet Training.
10. 45a.m. -	11. 45a.m.	Musketry. (Fire positions - Recognition of Targets - Bolt Drill.
12. 0noon -	12. 30p.m.	Gas Drill and Training.
2. 0p.m. -	3. 30p.m.	Lewis Gun Training.

4. **STEEL HELMETS**
    Care will be taken to preserve paint and Divisional Marking on Steel Helmets.
    Whilst in Billets Helmets will be hung up with equipment.

                                                P Darlington 2/Lieut.,
                                                Acting Adjutant,
                       9th. Battalion The Manchester Regiment.

Appendix 'G'

BATTALION ORDERS   No. 14
BY
LIEUT-COLONEL J. L. HESELTON, D.S.O., M.C.   Tuesday
COMMANDING 9TH. BATTALION THE MANCHESTER REGIMENT.
                                                  14. 5. 18.

Orderly Officer :-

2/Lieut. A. V. Hedges, M. C.

---

1. **REVEILLE**
   Reveille at 6. 30a.m.
2. **BREAKFASTS**
   Breakfasts at 7. 30a.m.
3. **PARADES**
   N. C. Os. and men not affected by moves in para. 4. will parade at 9. 0a.m.
4. **MOVE**
   (a) O. C. "A" Company   - Capt. R.E. King,

C.S.M.	- 351033	C.S.M. Travis, R.
C.Q.M.S.	- 14178	C.Q.M.S. Whitehead, H.
Gas Instructor	- 351014	Cpl. Morris, T.
Lewis G. Instructor	- 351327	Pte. Holt, H.
Batman	- 350724	" Hall, H.

   The above mentioned Company Cadre will move to FRIRUELLES tomorrow for attachment to the Company of 2nd. Bn., 327th. Regt. billeted there.

   (b) O. C. "B" Company   - Lieut. A.E. Statham,

C. S. M.	- 351419	C. S. M. Lawler
C. Q. M. S.	- 351036	C.Q.M.S. Calvert, W.
Gas Instructor	- 350459	Cpl. Gorman, F.
Lewis G. Instructor	- 201970	Pte. Strettle, E.
Batman	- 10141	" Hart, W.

   The above mentioned Company Cadre will move to CAMPAGNE tomorrow for attachment to the Company of 2nd. Bn. 327th. Regt. billeted there.

   The above moves to be complete by 10. 0a.m.
   Mess Cart will deliver Officers' Kits before 3. 0p.m.

   O. C. "A" and "B" Companies are responsible for the furnishing of sufficient guides who are familiar with the billets of their respective villages, to meet the incoming Companies of 2nd. Battn. 327th. Regt.

5. **RATIONS**
   Quartermaster will arrange for rationing of detached Company Cadres.
6. **DISCIPLINE**
   Attention must be paid to the saluting of N.C.Os. and men of the Battalion Cadre. It must at all times be smart,

   When moving about outside billets Officers servants and employed men must be properly dressed, wearing both belts and puttees.

BATTALION ORDERS (Continued).   No. 14.
----

7. INCREASE
           2/Lieut. O. HAMILTON reported from Hospital
           and is posted to " C" Company.

8. COURSES
           2/Lieut. A. G. SHILLINGLAW will proceed to attend
           a Lewis Gun Course at LE TOUQUET, assembling
           16th. inst.

                    --------- ---------

                                    P Darlington
                                              2/Lieut.,
                                        Acting Adjutant,
                            9th. Battalion The Manchester Regiment.

Appendix 'G'

BATTALION ORDERS   No. 15
                BY
LIEUT-COLONEL J. L. HESELTON, D.S.O., M.C.   Wednesday
COMMANDING 9TH. BATTALION THE MANCHESTER REGIMENT.
                                                              15.5.18.

Orderly Officer :-

2/Lieut. A. V. Hedges, M.C.

1. REVEILLE
   Reveille at 6.30a.m.

2. BREAKFASTS
   Breakfasts at 7.30a.m.

3. PARADES
   Parade at 9.0a.m.
   Dress :- Belt and Bayonet.

4. CASH
   2/Lieut. E. Porter, M.M., will report to
   Battalion Orderly Room at 9.0a.m. for the
   purpose of drawing Company Cash.

5. DISCIPLINE
   Sticks, if carried by W.Os. N.C.Os. and men
   must be of the regulation pattern, i.e.
   W.Os. Class I.-
   Knobbed walking stick.
   Other ranks, - Short Cane.

6. COURSE
   Para. 8. Battalion Orders No. 14 is cancelled.
   This Course will not take place.

                                    (Signed) P. DARLINGTON,
                                              2/Lieut.,
                                          Acting Adjutant,
                                9th. Battalion The Manchester Regiment.

APPENDIX "G"

BATTALION ORDERS   No. 16
BY
LIEUT-COLONEL J. L. KNOWLTON, D.S.O., M.C.   Thursday
COMMANDING 9TH. BATTALION THE MANCHESTER REGIMENT.
                                                 16. 5. 18.

==

Orderly Officer :-

    2/Lieut. A. F. Hodges, M.C.

==

1. **REVEILLE**
       Reveille at 6. 30a.m.

2. **BREAKFASTS**
       Breakfasts at 7. 3oa.m.

3. **PARADES**
       Parade at 8. 50a.m.   Fall in at 9. 0a.m.
       Dress :- Drill Order and Rifle.

       9. 0a.m. - 9. 15a.m.   Inspection.

       9. 30a.m. - 10. 30a.m. Physical Training
                               and Bayonet Training.

       10. 45a.m.- 11. 45a.m. Musketry.
                               (Holt Drill - Loading
                               and Firing Positions -
                               Recognition of Targets.

       12. Onoon - 12. 30p.m. Small Box Respirator Drill

4. **SICK**
       Sick to parade at Battalion Orderly Room at
       10. 15a.m.
       Sick report will be handed in to Battalion Orderly
       Room by 9. 30a.m. each morning.

5. **DISCIPLINE**
       All ranks must be in billets by 9. 30p.m.

6. **TEMPORARY ATTACHMENT**
       No. 36668 Cpl. Chadderton, R., M.M., will report
       to Capt. H. E. KING, at BRINCAMPS by 9. 0a.m.
       to-day 16th. inst.   To be accommodated and
       rationed by "A" Company from the 17th. inst.
       Full kit will be taken.

==

                           (Signed) F. DuDDLESTON,
                                    2/Lieut.,
                                    Acting Adjutant,
                       9th. Battalion The Manchester Regiment.

APPENDIX "G"

BATTALION ORDERS
BY
LIEUT-COLONEL. J. L. KNOTT, D.S.O., M.C.   No. 98
COMMANDING 9TH. BATTALION THE MANCHESTER REGIMENT.   Saturday
                                                      15. 3. 19.

Orderly Officer :-

2/Lieut. A. V. Hedges, M.C.

1. **REVEILLE**
   Reveille at 6.30a.m.

2. **BREAKFASTS**
   Breakfasts at 7. 00a.m.

3. **DINNERS**
   Dinners at 12. 15p.m.

4. **PARADES**
   The undermentioned O.Ranks will report
   to 2nd. Battalion 307th. Regiment as under
   at 8. 0a.m. on parade ground and conform to
   American Training hours.

   "C" Company Cadre
        2/Lieut. Porter, L.

        350074 C.S.M Grantham, H.J.D.C.M.
        352215 Cpl. Smiley, L.C. Gas Instructor
        353305 Pte. Mason, J.   Lewis G. "
        351924 Sgt. Fairbrother, W. Musk. Instr.
        351724   "   Selling, J.   Lewis G. Instr.
        350455 Cpl. German, F.   Gas Instructor

   The above will report to "F" Company 2nd. Battn.
   307th. Regiment.

   "D" Company Cadre
        2/Lieut. E. Wilcock,

        350705 C.S.M. Martin, W.
        350715 L/Sgt. Howell, F. Gas Instructor
        54412   Pte.   Pratt,   Lewis Gun "
        351975   "   Smeathe, E.   "
        351724 Sergt. Hilliton, H.   "
        350969 Cpl.   Smiley, W. Musky. Instr.

   The above will report to "G" Company 2nd.
   Battalion 307th. Regiment.

   352714 Sergt. Moss, J. D.C.M., will report
   to senior American Officer at 8. 0a.m. to instruct
   in Physical Training and Bayonet Training.

   DRESS :- Musketry Instructors - Drill Order &
                                       Rifle.
               Lewis Gun   "   - Belt and Bayonet
               Gas   "   - "   "   "

   Lieut. A. J. STANWAY, C. S. M. Billings, C.R.
   and C.S.M. Lawler, M., will meet working party of
   2nd. Battalion at American Battalion Headquarters
   at 8. 0a.m. for work on Assault Course. Working
   party will be complete with tools.

   2/Lieut. A. G. Shillinglaw will take American
   Officers in Lewis Gun at 2. 0p.m. behind
   9th. Manchester Headquarters.
   2/Lieut. A. G. Shillinglaw will provide Lewis Gun.

APPENDIX 'G'

BATTALION ORDERS (Continued).   No. 15.

5. **DISCIPLINE**
    O. C. Companies are held responsible that
    instructors report at the proper time and
    conform to American Training hours. No
    British Instructor must consider himself
    dismissed without the sanction of his O.C.
    Company.

                            (Signed) F. Richardson,
                                Captain & Adjutant,
                    9th. Battalion The Manchester Regiment.

APPENDIX 'G'

BATTALION ORDERS   No. 19
BY
LIEUT-COLONEL J. L. HESELTON, D.S.O., M.C.   Sunday
COMMANDING 9TH. BATTALION THE MANCHESTER REGIMENT.
                                              19. 5. 19.

Orderly Officer :-

    2/Lieut. A. V. Hedges, M.C.,

1 REVEILLE
    Reveille at 6. 30.a.m.
2 BREAKFASTS
    Breakfasts at 7. 30a.m.
3 PARADES
    Officers and N. C. Os. attached to American Working Parties will parade with same Working Parties as for to-day, at 8. 30a.m. on respective tasks.

Church Parade
    R.Cs. will parade for service at Church, FRANLEU, at 10. 0a.m.

Medical Inpsection.
    All W.Os., N.C.Os. and men not employed in para. 4, but including Regimentally employed, will parade at 10. 30a.m. in Cadre Billet for Medical Inspection.
    The R.S.M. will be responsible for this parade.

                      (Signed) P. DARLINGTON,
                                Captain,
                                Adjutant,
        9th. Battalion The Manchester Rgt.

Distribution :-

    O. C. 2nd. Battn. 327th. Regt.
    O. C. "E" Coy.   "   "
    O. C. "G" Coy.   "   "
    The Commanding Officer
    O. C. "A" Company,
    O. C. "B" Company,
    O. C. "C" Company,
    O. C. "D" Company,
    The R.S.M.
    File.

APPENDIX 'G'

BATTALION ORDERS No. ...
BY
LT. COLONEL J. L. HIRBIES, D...O., ...C. Sunday
COMMANDING 9TH. BATTALION THE MANCHESTER REGIMENT.
26. 5. 18.

Orderly Officer :-

2/Lieut. A. V. Hedges, M.C.

1. **REVEILLE**
   Reveille at 6.30a.m.

2. **BREAKFASTS**
   Breakfasts at 7.0a.m.

3. **PARADES**
   "A" Company Cadre will report to "F" Company
   2nd. Battn. 327th. Regt., (PRISONIERS) at
   8. 0a.m.

   "A" Company Cadre
   Capt. E. N. King,

   351035 C.S.M. Frayle, A.
   351724 Sgt.   Collins, J.   Lewis Gun Instructor
   351887 Pte.   Holt, H.   "   "   "
   340807 Cpl.   Chadderton, E., M.M. Musky."
   351644   "   Morris, G.   Gas Instructor.

   "B" Company Cadre will report to "G" Company
   2nd. Battn. 327th. Regt., (PRANLEU) at 8. 0a.m.

   "B" Company Cadre
   2/Lieut. C. Hamilton,

   350074 C.S.M. Grantham, D.C.M.
   350312 Cpl.   Hoyle, L.   Lewis G. Instructor
   351970 Pte.   Strettle, E.   "   "   "
   351914 Sgt.   Fairbrother, R. Musketry Instr.
   350715 Cpl.   Ratley, M.C.   Gas Instructor

   "D" Company Cadre will report to "E" Company
   2nd. Battn. 327th. Regt., (PRANLEU) at 8. 0a.m.

   "D" Company Cadre
   2/Lieut. H. Silcock

   350703 C.S.M. Martin, W.
   352565 Sgt.   Hillitch, H.   Lewis G. Instructor
   352535 L/Cpl. McCoy, J.   "   "   "
   350715 L/Sgt. Newall, F.   Gas Instructor
   352368 Sgt.   Outram, J.   Musketry Instructor
   350969 Cpl.   Smalley, A.   "   "

   Lieut. A. J. STATHAM, C.S.M. Lawler, R.,
   Sergt. G. Warren, and Sgt. Ross, J., will
   supervise work on assault course.

   O. C. Companies are responsible that
   Cadres are on their respective parade grounds
   to time.

   (Signed) F. BARLINGTON,
                Captain,
                Adjutant,
   9th. Battalion The Manchester Regiment.

Appendix 'G'

BATTALION ORDERS   No. 21
BY
LIEUT-COLONEL J. L. HAMILTON, D.S.O., M.C.   Tuesday
COMMANDING 9TH. BATTALION THE MANCHESTER REGIMENT.
                                                    21. 5. 18.

Orderly Officer :-

2/Lieut. A. C. Shillinglaw.

1. REVEILLE
   Reveille at 6. 30a.m.

2. BREAKFASTS
   Breakfasts at 7. 0a.m.

3. PARADES
   "A" Company Cadre will report to "F" Company
   2nd. Battn. 327th. Regt., (FRIBUELLES) at
   8. 0a.m.

   "A" Company Cadre

   Capt. R. R. King.

   351033   C.S.M.   Travis, R.
   351724   Sgt.   Mellins, J., Lewis Gun Instructor
   351327   Pte.   Holt, H.   "   "   "
   350680   Cpl.   Chadderton, R., M.M. Musky. Instr.
   351044   "   Morris, C.   Gas Instructor.

   "C" Company Cadre will report to "G" Company
   2nd. Battn. 327th. Regiment., (FRANLEU), at
   8. 0a.m.

   "C" Company Cadre

   2/Lieut. C. Hamilton.

   350074   C.S.M.   Grantham, H., D.C.M.
   350312   Cpl.   Sayle, T.   Lewis Gun Instructor
   201970   Pte.   Strettle, E.   "   "   "
   351912   Sgt.   Fairbrother, R. Musky. Instructor
   350218   Cpl.   Matley, H.C.   Gas Instructor.

   "D" Company Cadre will report to "E" Company
   2nd. Battn. 397th. Regiment., (FRANLEU) at
   8. 0a.m.

   "D" Company Cadre

   2/Lieut. N. Wilcock

   350705   C.S.M.   Martin, W.
   362565   Sgt.   Hilditch, H.   Lewis Gun Instructor
   352835   L/Cpl.   McCoy, T.   "   "   "
   350718   L/Sgt.   Newall, F.   Gas Instructor
   352868   Sgt.   Outram, J.   Musketry Instructor
   200969   Cpl.   Smalley, W.   "   "

                Lieut. A. J. STATHAM, C.S.M. Lawler, H.
   Sergt. G. Warren., Sergt. J. Moss, will supervise
   work on assault course.

                        (Signed) P. DARLINGTON,
                                    Captain,
                                    Adjutant,
                        9th. Battalion The Manchester Regt.

APPENDIX 'G'

BATTALION ORDERS
BY
LIEUT-COLONEL J. L. HESELTON, D.S.O., M.C.
COMMANDING 9TH. BATTALION THE MANCHESTER REGIMENT.

No 24
Friday
24. 5. 18

Orderly Officer:-

    2/Lieut. A. G. Shillinglaw.

1. REVEILLE
    Reveille at 6. 30 a.m.
2. BREAKFASTS
    Breakfasts at 7. 0a.m.
3. SICK PARADE
    Sick parade at 7. 30a.m. at American Infirmary.
4. PARADES
    Company Cadres will parade as for yesterday.

    (Signed) P. DARLINGTON,
    Captain & Adjutant,
9th. Battalion The Manchester Regiment.

Distribution :-
    2nd. Battn. 327th. Regt. (4 Copies).
    Commanding Officer
    O. C. "A" Company,
    O. C. "B" Company,
    O. C. "C" Company,
    O. C. "D" Company.
    The R. S. M.
    File.

APPENDIX 'G'

BATTALION ORDERS
BY
LIEUT-COLONEL J. L. HAMILTON, D.S.O., M.C.
COMMANDING 9TH. BATTALION THE MANCHESTER REGIMENT. 27. 5. 18

1. **REVEILLE**
   Reveille at xxxxxxxx. 6. 0a.m.

2. **BREAKFASTS**
   Breakfasts at xxxxxxxx 6. 15a.m.

3. **PARADES**
   Cadres as under, will report to 3rd. Battalion.
   328th. Regt. Headquarters at xxxxxxx. 6. 55a.m.

   "C" Company Cadre will report to "I" & "K" Companies.

   "C" Company Cadre

   2/Lieut. C. Hamilton,

380074	C.S.M.	Grantham, H., D.C.M.	
350118	Cpl.	Oakley, S.C.	Gas Instructor
350312	"	Doyle, T.	L.G. Instructor
351914	Sgt.	Fairbrother, H.	Musketry Instructor
43100	Cpl.	Dawson, B.	Bombing Instructor.

   "D" Company Cadre will report to "L" & "M" Companies.

   "D" Company Cadre
   2/Lieut. F. Wilcock,

12/147	R.S.M.	Temple, H.	
354705	C.S.M.	Martin, W.	
350718	L/Sgt.	Newall, V.	Gas Instructor
352566	Sgt.	Hilditch, H.	L.G. Instructor
352836	L/Cpl.	McCoy, J.	
352082	Sgt.	Outram, J.	Musketry Instructor

   No. 11612 Sergt. Warren, J. will parade with
   "C" Company Cadre.

   DRESS :- Musketry Instructors - Drill Order and
                                           Rifle.
           Gas Instructors   - Belt and Bayonet
                                    and S. B. R.
           Lewis Gun Instrs.   - Belt and Bayonet.

   Haversack Rations will be carried. Dinners will
   be had on return to Billets.

   All men will wear ground sheets rolled at the
   back of belt.

   (Signed) F. HARRINGTON,
                     Captain,
                     Adjutant,
           9th. Battalion The Manchester Regiment.

Distribution :-
    O. C. 3rd. Battn. 328th. Regt. (4 copies).
    Commanding Officer
    O. C. "A" Company,
    O. C. "B" Company,
    O. C. "C" Company,
    O. C. "D" Company,
    The R. S. M.
    File.

APPENDIX 'G'

BATTALION ORDERS
BY
LIEUT-COLONEL J. L. HAMILTON, D.S.O., M.C.
COMMANDING 9TH. BATTALION THE MANCHESTER REGIMENT.

Tuesday
28. 5. 18

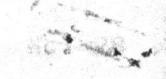

Orderly Officer :-

2/Lieut. O. Hamilton.

---

1. **REVEILLE**
   Reveille at 6. 0a.m.

2. **BREAKFASTS**
   Breakfasts at 6. 15a.m.

3. **PARADES**
   Cadres as under will report to 3rd. Battalion
   328th. Regiment Headquarters at 6. 55a.m.

   "C" Company Cadre will report to "I" & "K" Companies.

   "C" Company Cadre

   Lieut. W. O. Hickson,

   350074 C. S. M. Grantham, H. D.C.M.
   350215 Cpl.   Matley, E. C. Gas Instructor
   350312   "   Gayle,   T.   L. G.   "
   351914 Sgt.   Fairbrother, M. Musketry   "
    43100 Cpl.   Dawson, H.   Bombing   "

   11812   Sgt.   Warren, J. will parade with
   "C" Company Cadre.

   "D" Company Cadre will report to "L" and "M" Companies.

   "D" Company Cadre

   2/Lieut. H. Wilcock,

   12/147 R. S. M. Temple, R.
   350705 C. S. M. Martin, W.
   350714 L/Sgt. Newall, F.   Gas Instructor
   352566 Sgt.   Hilditch, M. M.C.   "
   352833 L/Cpl. McCoy, J.   "
   350063 Sgt.   Outram, J.   Musketry "

   DRESS :- Musketry Instructors - Drill Order and Rifle
            Gas Instructors   - Belt & Bayonet &
                                    S. B. R.
            Lewis Gun   "   - Belt and Bayonet.

            All men will wear ground sheets rolled at
   the back of belt.
            Haversack rations will be carried.

4. **CASH**
   Officers requiring cash will hand in advance books
   to Battalion Orderly Room by 9. 0a.m.
   The Orderly Officer will report to Battalion
   Orderly Room at 9. 0a.m. for instructions regarding
   drawing of cash.

(Signed) F. DARLINGTON.
Captain,
Adjutant,
9th. Battalion The Manchester

Army Form C. 2118.

9 Manchester R.
Vol. 16

WAR DIARY
or
INTELLIGENCE SUMMARY.

(Erase heading not required.)

Instructions regarding War Diaries and Intelligence Summaries are contained in F. S. Regs., Part II. and the Staff Manual respectively. Title pages will be prepared in manuscript.

Place	Date	Hour	Summary of Events and Information	Remarks and references to Appendices
FRANLEU	JUNE 1st		Headquarters and "D" Company Cadre remained at FRANLEU attached to 2nd Battalion 327th Regiment.	
	2nd		"A" Company Cadre remained at FRIKVELLES attached to "F" Coy 2nd Bath. 327th Regiment.	
	3rd		"B" and "C" Companies remained at LAMBERCOURT attached to 2nd Battalion, 327th Regiment.	
	4th		Cadres assisted in training their respective affiliated American Units.	
	5th			
WOIGNARUE 6th			Headquarters "A" and "D" Company Cadres moved to WOIGNARUE (Ref. Sheet ABBEVILLE 14·1/100,000) and were attached to 1st Bath. 326th. Regt. "B" and "C" Company Cadres moved to ONIVAL and were attached to 2nd. Battalion 326th Regiment. For details of move see appendix "A"	APPENDIX "A"

Army Form C. 2118.

WAR DIARY
or
INTELLIGENCE SUMMARY.

(Erase heading not required.)

Place	Date	Hour	Summary of Events and Information	Remarks and references to Appendices
NOIGNARUE	JUNE 7th		Cadres located in training their respective affiliated American Unit, extensive training being given in Anti-Gas measures Musketry, P.T, B.T and assault.	
	8th			
	9th			
	10th			
	11th			
	12th			
	13th			
	14th			
ONIVAL	15th		Headquarters 'A' and 'D' Company Cadres moved to ONIVAL (Ref. Sheet. ABBEVILLE. 14. 1/100,000) and were established in camp with 'B' & 'C' Coy. Cadres.	

WAR DIARY
or
INTELLIGENCE SUMMARY.
(Erase heading not required.)

Army Form C. 2118.

Place	Date	Hour	Summary of Events and Information	Remarks and references to Appendices
ONIVAL	JUNE 15th	4.30 p.m.	2nd Battn. 107th Regt. arrived at ONIVAL about 4.30 p.m. Battalion cadre attached to 2nd Battn. 107th Regt. for training purposes.	Ref Sheet ABBEVILLE 11H, 1/100,000
	16th 17th 18th		Cadres assisted in training 2nd Battn. 107th Regiment.	
PENDE	19th		Headquarters and "A" and "C" Company cadres moved by Route march to PENDE and became attached to 2nd Battn. 108th Regt. "B" and "D" Company cadres moved to BOUBERT and became attached to 1st. Battn. 108th Regt.	

Army Form C. 2118.

WAR DIARY
or
INTELLIGENCE SUMMARY.
(Erase heading not required.)

Place	Date	Hour	Summary of Events and Information	Remarks and references to Appendices
	JUNE			
PENDE	20th		Cadres assisted in training their affiliated American Unit.	
HAUTVILLERS	21st		Headquarters 'A' and 'C' Company Cadres moved by route march with 2nd Batn. 108th Regt. to HAUTVILLERS and were established in Billets there. 'B' and 'D' Company Cadres moved by route march with 1st Batn. 108th Regt. to DRUCAT.	Ref. Sheet ABBEVILLE 1/100,000 1/2/7
IVERGNY	22nd		Cadres moved with their respective affiliated American Units by lorry to :- Headquarters, 'A' and 'C' by Cadres - IVERGNY 'B' and 'D' Company Cadres - SUS ST LEGER	Ref. Sheet LENS 1/100, XP Jun

WAR DIARY
or
INTELLIGENCE SUMMARY

Army Form C. 2118.

Place	Date	Hour	Summary of Events and Information	Remarks and references to Appendices
	JUNE			
IVERGNY	23rd		Cadres assisted in training their affiliated American Units.	
	24th			
	25th		Training. G.H.Q. Line was reconnoitred with representatives of American Units.	
	26th			
PIERREGOT	27th		Batt. Cadre complete moved by Lorry to PIERREGOT and became Cadre in Brigade Reserve.	Ref Sheet LENS 1/100,000
	28th		Cadre carried out reconnaissance of all training grounds, Ranges etc, in this area. Reserve Trench Roads, tracks etc leading to same were also reconnoitred.	

Army Form C. 2118.

WAR DIARY
or
INTELLIGENCE SUMMARY.
(Erase heading not required.)

Place	Date	Hour	Summary of Events and Information	Remarks and references to Appendices
	JUNE			
PIERREGOT	29th		Party of Officer W. Os. and N. C. Os. thoroughly reconnoitred VADEN Line.	
	30th		Church Service. Reconnoitring of Area.	

APPENDIX 'A'
SECRET   Copy No. 14

9TH. BATTALION THE MANCHESTER REGIMENT

ORDER NO. 15

dated 6th. June, 1918.

Reference Sheet, ABBEVILLE 14, 1/100,000

Breakfast	Breakfasts at 6.30a.m.
Move	The Battalion will relieve 2/7th. Manchester Regt. in the WOIGNARUE and ONIVAL Area tomorrow the 7th. inst.
Route	FRANLEU - OCHANCOURT - NIBAS - BOURSEVILLE - WOIGNARUE - ONIVAL.
Parade	Battalion Cadre (less 2 Companies) will move to WOINNARUE and will parade in front of Battalion Orderly Room at 9.0a.m.
Blankets	Blankets rolled in bundles of ten will be handed in to the Quartermaster's Store at 7.0a.m.
Officer's Valises & Mess Kits	Officer's Kits and Mess Kits will be handed in to the Quartermaster's Store by 7.30a.m.
"B" & "C" Companies	"B" and "C" Company Cadres under Lieut. A. J. STATHAM will move to ONIVAL.
Parade	Parade at 6.45a.m. and meet H.Q. and "A" and "D" Companies in front of Battalion Orderly Room at FRANLEU.
Transport	Lieut. A. J. STATHAM will arrange for the loan of one limber from 3rd. Battalion 327th. Regiment for transportation of Blankets and Officer's Kits to FRANLEU where Kits etc. will be transferred to Baggage wagons. Quartermaster will arrange for collection of Blankets and Kits of "A" Company at FRIRUELLES by 7.30a.m.
Billets	2/Lieut. O. Hamilton will proceed to ONIVAL arriving at 11.0a.m. 2/Lieut. H. Tilcock will proceed to WOIGNARUE arriving by 10.30a.m.

P. Darlington Captain,
Adjutant,
9th. Battalion The Manchester Regiment.

Distribution :-
1 Officer Commanding 2nd. Battn. 327th. Rgt.
2. Commanding Officer
3 O. C. "A" Company,   7   2/Lieut. O. Hamilton,
4 O. C. "B" Company,   8   Quartermaster,
5 O. C. "C" Company   9   The R. S. M.
6 O. C. "D" Company.   10 R. Q. M. S.
                        11 & 12   War Diary
                           13   File.

CONFIDENTIAL

WAR DIARY
OF
9TH BATTALION THE MANCHESTER REGT.

FROM 1-7-1918
TO 31-7-1918

VOL. VI.

Army Form C. 2118.

WAR DIARY
or
INTELLIGENCE SUMMARY.

(Erase heading not required.)

WAR DIARY
of
2nd BATTALION HQ
MANCHESTER REGT.
1st September – 30th September 1918
Vol 1

Army Form C. 2118.

WAR DIARY
or
INTELLIGENCE SUMMARY.

(Erase heading not required.)

Instructions regarding War Diaries and Intelligence Summaries are contained in F. S. Regs., Part II and the Staff Manual respectively. Title pages will be prepared in manuscript.

Place	Date	Hour	Summary of Events and Information	Remarks and references to Appendices
PIERREGOT	JULY			
	1st		Battalion Cadre remained at PIERREGOT in Brigade Reserve and carried out training and the Reconnaissance of Corps Area and French System.	
	2nd			
	3rd		Attached to 124th Machine Gun Company, American troops for instructional purposes. Carried out training & Reconnaissance	
	4th			
	5th			
	6th			
	7th			
	8th			
	9th			
	10th			

WAR DIARY
or
INTELLIGENCE SUMMARY.

Army Form C. 2118.

Place	Date	Hour	Summary of Events and Information	Remarks and references to Appendices
IERREGNY	JULY			Ref Sheet
	11th		Men moved out. Training and Reconnaissance.	
	12th			
	13th			
	14th			ABBEVILLE 1/150,000
	15th		Bar. moved to BERTEAUCOURT staying there the night 15/16th in Billets.	do.
	16th		Bar. moved by Route March to PONT REMY and was established in Camp there.	
	17th		Men carried out Training at PONT REMY.	
	18th			
	19th			
	20th		Range Firing Competition, held by 199 Inf Brigade. There won 4 of 7 events.	
	21st			

Army Form C. 2118.

WAR DIARY
or
INTELLIGENCE SUMMARY.
(Erase heading not required.)

Place	Date	Hour	Summary of Events and Information	Remarks and references to Appendices
HAUDRICOURT	JULY			
	22nd		Cadre moved to HAUDRICOURT, entrained at PONT REMY and detrained at ABANCOURT.	Ref A.F.W. DIEPPE 1/100,000
	23rd			
	24th			
	25th			
	26th		Cadre carried out training.	
	27th			
	28th			
	29th			
	30th			
	31st			

CONFIDENTIAL

WAR DIARY

OF

13th (S) Bn. MANCHESTER REGT. (1st to 13th AUGUST 1918)
& Bn. MANCHESTER REGT. (14th to 31st AUGUST 1918)

FROM 1st to 31st AUGUST 1918

VOLUME No. 4 - No. 8.

Army Form C. 2113.

WAR DIARY

INTELLIGENCE SUMMARY

(Erase heading not required)

August 1918   13(S) Bn. The Manchester Regt

Place	Date	Hour	Summary of Events and Information	Remarks and references to Appendices
HAUDRICOURT, FRANCE DIEPPE 1:100,000	1-8-18		Training as per programme (Appendix No 3 of War Diary for July 1918) MAJOR J.S. SMYLIE proceeded on leave. (CAPT (ADJUTANT) L.A. TURVEY returned from leave. The Earl of DENBIGH lectured to all Officers and N.C.Os of the Brigade on the German War Aims", a most instructive interesting lecture. Honours granted and gazetted July 1918. The following N.C.Os were mentioned in Depatches in LONDON GAZETTE of Jany 3rd 1918 published in the TIMES of June 29.1918:- No 6836. Sgt ARNOLD A.G. "B" Coy. No 16267 L. Sgt KAY A.E. "B" Coy. and No 5741 Cpl LYONS J. "D" Coy. 2/Lieut J.H. HODGES and 1 O.R struck off the effective strength on admission to hospital with effect from 31-7-18.	Appendix No 1
-do-	2-8-18		Training etc as per programme. 10 OR struck off effective strength on admission to hospital from 1-8-18. MT. S.S.MVSE leave to U.K	
-do-	3-8-18		10 OR. from 2-8-18. 10 OR Living signal establishment effective strength from 1-8-18. The Battalion was inspected by the Divisional Commander Brig Gen BETHELL CMG, D.S.O. after which the lines were inspected. 5 OR struck off effective strength to hospital from 2-8-18 and 3-8-18. Extract from London Gazette 6 30991 dt 12th July 1918. That V.H.P. deJONGH to be 2nd Lieut (Regular Army) from Spec Reserve with seniority 15th Jan 1917. 2nd Lieut T SCHOFIELD leave to U.K.	Appendix No 1
-do-	4-8-18		Special Brigade Commemoration Service. Programme of Training and Work (Appendix No 1) incorporated Council 5th to 11th August 1918. 10 OR admitted in item 2 from 3-8-18. CAPT W.R BRITTINE leave to U.K.	Appendix 1
-do-	5-8-18		Training etc as per programme effective strength with effect from 4-8-18 one marked to 25 Stationary Hospital ROUEN Special Order of the day from F.M Marshall Sgt D AAIG. KT S.S.B. G.C.V.O. K.C.I.E. to the troops on the occasion of the 4th anniversary of the war 1 R.A.M.C. other ranks CAPT E.T.TAYLOR M.C returned from leave to U.K.	

Army Form C. 2118.

WAR DIARY
INTELLIGENCE SUMMARY.
(Erase heading not required.)

August 1918. 18/3(5)6th Bn Manchester Regt

Place	Date	Hour	Summary of Events and Information	Remarks and references to Appendices
HAUDRICOURT	6-8-18		Training and Work as per programme. 3 O.R. struck off effective strength after 14 days in hospital with effect from 6-5-18. 2nd Lieut R.H. ALLEN and 2nd Lieut J. BYRNE returned from RAINNEVILLE	FRANCE DIEPPE 16 1:100,000
"	7-8-18		Training etc as per programme. 1 O.R. having reported is taken on strength from 6-8-18.	
"	8-8-18 -2		Training etc as per programme. Lieut Col R.B. CAMPBELL D.S.O. D.L.F. Rgt Proceeded to the Brigade on the Bayonet. 2nd Lieut C.E. & B MORRELL N.V.O. proceeded on leave to U.K.	
"	9-8-18		Training etc as per programme. From 1st Aug 1918 the award of the military medal is extended to Warrant Officers Class I and II, conditions of award being the same as any one of N.C.Os and men. 2 O.R. struck off effective strength after 14 days in hospital with effect from 2-8-18. 1 O.R. having reported is taken on strength from 9-8-18.	
"	10-8-18		Training etc as per programme. 5 O.R. struck off effective strength after 14 days in hospital with effect from 10-8-18. A/RQM.S. G.WES admitted to hospital from base to U.K.	
"	11-8-18		Church Service as usual. Programme of training and work (August 18) issued (September 18) Appendix 03	
"	12-8-18		Training and work as per programme. 5 O.R. having reported are again taken on from 12-8-18. 1 O.R. struck off effective strength on evacuation to No. 3 Stat. Hospital ROUEN. 2nd Lieut H. SMITH returned from leave to U.K. 2nd Lieut C.F. GROVES and F.J. TURNER R. proceeded on leave to U.K.	

Army Form C. 2118.

WAR DIARY

INTELLIGENCE SUMMARY

1/3/5 Bn. Manchester Regt.

August 1918.

Place	Date	Hour	Summary of Events and Information	Remarks and references to Appendices
HAUDRICOURT	13-8-18		Work and Training in Programme. Programme for Training and Sports for 14th & 15th not issued. (Appendix No 2) CAPT CARTMAN and 17 O.R. (late 1/8 Bn) 2/Lt. ?for Bn.) Batty.?? commencing will in future be granted men on leave. The 1/5 (S) Bn. Manchester Regt. was absorbed by the 9/5 (T) Bn. Manchester Regt. at midnight 13/14/8/18 in accordance with 654 Army Routine Order No. 9984/ad.G.1 (A.G.I) dtd 2/8/18. The amalgamation is to be known as the 1/5 Bn. The Manchester Regt. All ranks are being transferred to the amalgamated Bn. Capt. P. DARLINGTON M.C. and Capt. R.H. KING (1/4 1/7) Bn. Manchester Regt.) are struck off duty from strength (1/8 1/7 Manchester Regt.) as taken on ration strength to "D" Coy. 23 O.R. are taken on from 30-7-18. 2/Lieut S.E. GWINNELL proceeded on leave to U.K. 2/Lieut J. FAZACKERLEY reported from leave to U.K. 2/Lieut O HNS M.G. ??? on leave to U.K. Training and work as per programme.	Not Issued FRANCE DIEPPE 1/6 1:100,000. Appendix 3.
—do—	14-8-18			
—do—	15-8-18		Training and work as per programme. Programme of Training and Work for 16th & 17th not issued. (Appendix No 4) Capt. E.H. COYNE M.C. (M.O.) returned from leave to U.K. was Lieut. G.A. ROBERTSON. Following Officers from 17th Bn (late) are taken on strength and posted to Coys as under. 4/Lieut F. RODDY M.C. D.C.M. "A" Coy. Lieut C. HILL M.C. "D" Coy. 2/Lieut R. HALLIDAY "D" Coy with effect from 30-7-18. 2/Lieut E. HALLIDAY to Coy. with effect from 18-3-18. 2/0 R attached off to Base. And at Board with effect from 11-8-18/3/8 Ba Reinforcements arrived 20/8/18. Following 1/4 became effective off the strength.	Appendix 4.
—do—	16-8-18		Training and work as per programme. 1 O.R. struck off effective strength work w.e.f. from 12-8-18 to 7/8/18 in hospital. And grievance return to duty details	

WAR DIARY or INTELLIGENCE SUMMARY

Army Form C. 2118.

(Erase heading not required.) 1/4 9th Bn The Manchester Regt

August 1918

Place	Date	Hour	Summary of Events and Information	Remarks and references to Appendices
HAUDRICOURT	17-8-18		Training and Work as per programme. 10.R having regard is taken on from 16-8-18. 10.R with off effective strength on admission to hospital 5-8-18.	Refshit FRANCE DIEPPE 1/6 1:100,000
"	18-8-18		Church Service as usual. Programme of Training and Work for 19th and continued week ending to hour to U.R. Appendix 20 5. MAJOR J.S. SMYLIE rejoined from leave to U.R.	Appendix 5
"	19-8-18		Training and work per programme. "Lieut" J. SCHOFIELD rejoined from leave to U.R.	
"	20-8-18		Training and work as per programme. Programme of training and Work for 21st and 22nd unit issued. (Appendix 20 6)	Appendix 6
"	21-8-18		Training and work as per programme. The following Officers reported for duty and are taken on strength and posted to Coys as shown :— 2/Lieut W. F. LAIRD "D" Coy, 2/Lieut J.F. FOX "B" Coy 2/Lieut F. LEEAN "A" Coy. 10.R Having rejoined on return on from 21-8-18.	
"	22-8-18		Training and work as per programme. CAPT & Q. E. R. RAITH 8/0 attached for duty & LIEUT A.V. HEDGES, M.C. posted to this unit on attache to U.K. Programme of Training & Work for 23rd is issued. (Appendix 20 7)	Appendix 7
"	23-8-18		Training and work as per programme. Programme of training was made to 10.R Details off Effective Strength after 7 days in hospital, with effect from 15-8-18.	

Army Form C. 2118.

WAR DIARY
or
INTELLIGENCE SUMMARY.
(Erase heading not required.)

August 1918   9th Bn The Wiltshire Regt.

Place	Date	Hour	Summary of Events and Information	Remarks and references to Appendices
HAUDRICOURT	21-8-18		Lieut Col. J.F.S. MORRELL M.M.O returned from leave to U.K. 23-8-18. Visit to Bombing Course and Lectured School for Officers and N.C.O's. The undermentioned Officers & Junior N.C.O's taken on strength and posted to Coys shown. Lieut 23-7-18. Lieut J.A. STAYING No 24 FRANCE DIEPPE 16. 1:100,000 Lieut R.J.G. HIBBS "D" Coy 24/7 R.H.H DAVIES "D" Coy No 8169 R.H. NANER "A" 24.7.18. To O.R. 23.7.18 To O.R. A.S. [illegible] to Battalion strength[?] at H.Q of the Battalion 23-7-18 To O.R. having reported to duty and taken on strength	Appendix No 1. Appendix No 3
do	25.8.18		Usual Services as usual. Bayonet Training and Obstacles(?) for all (Appendix 3)	
do	26.8.18		15 yds and Training saw parties as for last week. W.O.R are [illegible] to take a state of the 4 O.R having been attached to hourly M.I.R [illegible] in strength to 4.O.R. Effective strength from 13-7-18 (absent from leave(?) and (in spine to H.Q) march Bn 275 and 100 Q. when arrived from 13-7-18, (absent T.M.B) 2/Lt F. TURNER attached from Hants to Bn.	Appendix No 9
do	27.8.18		Battalion carried on to finish Bomb course Officers and N.C.Os as first. At [illegible] on the Lewis C.F. BROWES returned from leave to U.K. Conference at 11.30 am at H.R. for Coy officers	
do	29.8.18		Battalion worked on bombing Course in C. Area. Junior Officers instruction in use of C.O Light German Musket to an Maj reading and mid[?] of Compass concluding with lecture by C.O. 2/O.R.I. having appointed on [illegible] on total [illegible] with effect from 27 & 8. 4.O.R are struck off after 3 days in hospital and struck off for various dates 2/Lieuts S.E GWINNELL and C. HILLMS reported from leave to U.K. Capt T. DARLINGTON MC proceeded on leave to U.K.	

Army Form C. 2118.

WAR DIARY
INTELLIGENCE SUMMARY.
(Erase heading not required.)

9th Bn The Manchester Regt

August 1918.

Place	Date	Hour	Summary of Events and Information	Remarks and references to Appendices
HAUDRICOURT	30-8-18		Training Musketry Specialists Anti Aircraft Lewis Gun, Young N.C.Os, Riding School for Officers. Tactical Scheme will be held on Wednesdays for all Officers, and on Saturday for all N.C.Os. 2nd Lieut J.H. HODGES invalided to UK 9-7-18, 3 OR invalided to UK between 4-8-18 and 14-8-18.	Maps France DIEPPE 16 1:100,000
do.	31-8-18		Battalion route march, kit and foot inspection. Scheme for platoon and section competition. The band instruments of the late 17th(S)Bn having arrived, a brass band is being formed in the Battalion. The health of the Battalion is good, a small proportion of the men on leave has had influenza but in the Battalion itself there have been very little. The effective strength of the Battalion is 46 Officers and 739 OR	
	1-9-18			

J.F.B. Morrell
Lieut Col
Cmdg 9th Bn The Manchester Regt.

Appendix No 1

Programme of Training & Work. 5th–11th Aug 1918

13th (S) BATTALION THE MANCHESTER REGIMENT.
PROGRAMME OF TRAINING & WORK.
for week ending 10th August 1918.

Day.	Hour.	TRAINING & WORK.
MONDAY, 5th Aug.	9.40 a.m.	G.O.C's (66th Div) Inspection of Battalion and Camp.
	11 - 12.45 p.m.	H.Q. & Coy. L.G. Classes firing on the 100 yds range.
	2.00 - 3.00 "	Specialist Training.
	1.30 - 4.30 "	"B" Coy. Firing on 100 yds Range. 5 rounds Grouping, 5 rounds Application.
	4.30 - 7.30 "	"C" Coy. do. do. do.
	1.30 - 4.30 "	"A" & "D" Coys. working on Assault Course and Bombing Trenches and Pits.
	5.00 "	G.O.C., 66th Div. Inspection of Reg. Transport.
	2.00 "	Quinine Parade for all men in Camp (remainder as arranged by Coys).
		Inter-Platoon knock-out Competition. 2nd Round.
TUESDAY. 6th Aug.	8.15 - 12.30 a.m.	"B" & "C" Coys. working on Assault and Bombing Courses.
	8.30 - 12.30 "	"A" Coy. firing on 100 yds Range. 5 rds Grouping., 5 rds Application.
	8.30 - 9.00 "	"D" Coy. P.T., also Specialists.
	9.15 - 10.30 "	"D" Coy. Inspection & Handling of Arms. Specialists Classes, training, Junior N.C.Os examination.
	12.00 - 12.30 p.m.	Specialist Training, and Gas Drill.
	1.45 "	Battalion Quinine Parade (All present).
	2.00 - 3.00 "	"A" Coy. Handling of Arms, Gas Drill, and Specialists Classes.
	2.00 - 5.00 "	"D" Coy. firing on 100 yds Range. 5 rds Grouping, 5 rds Application.
	6.00 "	Lecture by Brigade to all Officers & N.C.Os.
		Inter-Platoon Football Competition.
WEDNESDAY, 7th Aug.	8.15 - 9.00 a.m.	Adjutant's Parade for "B" & "C" Coys. & Specialists and new Junior N.C.Os. class.
	8.15 - 12.30 "	"A" & "D" Coys. working on Assault and Bombing Courses.
	9.30 - 12.30 "	"B" & "C" Coys. Platoon Training. Drill in Artillery formation and extension under new organisation (Area A.2). Specialist Classes. Training Junior N.C.Os. Class, Squad Drill, Gas, & P.T.
	2.00 p.m.	Battalion Quinine Parade (All present).
	6.00 "	Tactical Scheme for Coy. Officers & N.C.Os.
		Battalion Football Match (v 12th Lancs. Fus.)
THURSDAY, 8th Aug.	8.15 - 9.00 a.m.	AS FOR WEDNESDAY for "A" & "D", etc.,
	8.15 - 12.30 "	"B" & "C" Coys. working on Assault and Bombing Courses. (These works to be completed)
	9.30 - 12.30 "	"A" & "D" Coys. as for "B" & "C" Coys on WED'Y. Specialists Classes, training, Junior N.C.Os Class, B.T, Squad Drill, Musketry.
	2.00 p.m.	Battalion Quinine Parade (All present).
		Semi-finals. Platoon Football Competition.
FRIDAY. 9th Aug.	8.30 - 9.00 a.m.	P.T. All Coys. Specialists and Junior N.C.Os Classes.
	9.15 - 10.30 "	Coy. Inspection & Coy. Drill., Specialist Training, and Junior N.C.Os Class, Detail of handling of arms.
	11.00 - 11.45 "	Coys. Musketry, Rapid Loading etc. Specialist Training, Junior N.C.Os Class, B.T.
	12.00 - 12.45 p.m.	Coys. Gas Training, & Extensions in Gas Masks. Specialists Training in Gas Masks & Gas Drill. Junior N.C.Os Class, Map Reading, & use of Compass.
	2.00 "	Battalion Quinine Parade (All present).
	6.00 "	Lecture by Brigade to all Officers & N.C.Os.
		Boxing in the evening.

PROGRAMME OF TRAINING (CONTINUED).

Day.	Hour.	TRAINING & WORK.
	8.15 – 9.00 a.m.	Bayonet Training. All Specialists & Junior N.C.Os.
SATURDAY. 10th Aug.	9.30 – 12.30 "	Platoon Training in Drill of Artillery Formation and extension under new Organisation (C.1. Area). Specialist Classes Training, Junior N.C.Os Class, Platoon Drill, P.T., and Musketry.
	2.00 p.m.	Battalion Quinine Parade (All present).
	2.00 "	Tactical Scheme for all Coy. Officers & N.C.Os. on The Ground.
	6.00 "	Final of Inter-Platoon Football Competition
SUNDAY, 11th Aug.	MORNING.	Voluntary Church Parade and Domestic Fatigues
	AFTERNOON.	– RECREATION –

N.B., (1) When Companies are carrying out Platoon Training the trained Specialists will go with Platoons.

(2) When Companies are training on Areas where Assault Course and Bombing Pits are dug, B.T, Bombing, and Rifle Grenade training will be carried out.

L. A. Tuvey

Captain & Adjutant.
for Lieut. Colonel.
Comdg. 13th (S) Bn. Manchester Regt.

4/8/18.

Appendix no 2

Programme of Training and Work.
Aug 12th or 13th 1918

13th (S) BATTN. THE MANCHESTER REGT.
PROGRAMME OF TRAINING & WORK.

Day.	Hour.	TRAINING & WORK.
	8.15 – 12.30 a.m.	"A" & "D" Coys. Working on Assault Course.
	8.30 – 11.30 "	"B" Coy. (Musketry) Range. Bz
	2.00 – 5.00 p.m.	"C" " do. do. Bz
	2.00 – 3.00 "	"B" " Handling of Arms, Gas Drill * & Specialists.
	8.30 – 9.30 a.m.	"C" " Handling of Arms, Gas Drill * & Specialists.
MONDAY,	8.30 – 12.30 "	"H.Q." L.G. Section. Anti-Aircraft Course.
12th Aug.	12. noon.	"B" Coy. Quinine Parade.
	2.00 p.m.	Other Coys. " "
	8.30 – 9.00 a.m.)	
	9.15 – 10.30 ")	Junior N.C.Os., A.G.I., Bayonet Fighting,
	11.00 – 11.45 ")	P.T. Drill, Musketry.
	12.00 – 12.45 p.m.)	
		Riding School for Officers.
	5.00 p.m.	Recreational Training.
	6.00 "	Lecture for Officers & N.C.Os "Food Supplies"

* __Half-hour per 2 platoons Gas Instruction, under Gas N.C.Os.__

	8.15 – 12.30 a.m.	"B" & "C" Coys. Working on Assault Course.
	8.30 – 10.30 "	"A" Coy. (Musketry) Range. Bz
	10.30 – 12.30 "	"D" " do. do. Bz
TUESDAY.	8.30 – 9.30 "	"D" " Specialists, Handling of Arms, Gas Drill *
13th Aug.	10.30 – 11.30 "	"A" " do. do.
	9.30 – 10.30 "	"D" " Lecture on "Bombing" by Bombing Sgt.
	11.30 – 12.30 "	"A" " do. do.

P.T.O.

Day.	Hour.	TRAINING & WORK.
TUESDAY, 13th Aug.	8.30 – 12.30 a.m.	"H.Q." L.G. Section. Anti-Aircraft Course.
	3.30 p.m.	Quinine Parade (All Coys).
		Junior N.C.Os. as for MONDAY.
	2.00 "	Lecture for Officers & N.C.Os. "Map Reading" by G.O.C.,
		Recreational Training in afternoon.

* Half-hour per 2 platoons Gas Instruction under Gas N.C.Os.

L A Turney

Captain & Adjutant.
for Lieut. Colonel.
Comdg. 13th (S) Bn. Manchester Regiment.

11/8/18.

Appendix No. 3

Programme of Training and Work
August 14th & 15th 1918

Day.	Hour.	Training and work

THURSDAY

Aug 15th.

                ANTIBT

                ANTI-AIRCRAFT COURSE

                Specialists Classes.

                Junior N.C.Os Physical Training, Squad Drill, Bayonet Fighting, Musketry.

2.0.p.m. Battalion Quinine Parade.

6.0.p.m. Recreational Training - Inter Coy. League.

L A Turvey

                          Capt and Adjt.,
       13th Battalion, The Manchester Regiment.

13th August 1918

13th BATTN. THE MANCHESTER REGT.
PROGRAMME OF TRAINING AND WORK

Day.	Hour	TRAINING AND WORK

	8.15 - 12.30 p.m.	"A" & "D" Coys. Working on Assault and Bayonet Fighting Course.
WEDNESDAY	8.30 - 9.0 a.m.	"B" & "C" Coys. Physical Training.
	9.15 - 10.30 a.m.	"B" & "C" Coys. Drill, Rifle Exercise and extension in gas masks.
	11.0 - 11.45 a.m.	"B" Coy — Musketry Instruction
14th Aug.	12.0 - 12.45 p.m.	"B" Coy — Bombing Lecture.
	11.0 - 11.45 a.m.	"C" Coy — Bombing Lecture.
	12.0 - 12.45 p.m.	"C" Coy — Musketry Instruction.

ANTI AIRCRAFT COURSE   —   Specialists Classes.

Training Junior N.C.Os
 8.30 - 9.0   Physical Training
 9.15 - 10.30 am   Detail of handling Arms.
 11.0 - 11.45 am   Bayonet Fighting.
 12.0 - 12.45   Map Reading and use of compass.

 2. p.m.   Battalion Quinine Parade

 6.0. p.m.   Tactical Scheme for Coy. Officers and N.C.Os
              Recreational Training — Inter Coy. League.

| THURSDAY | 8.15. - 12.30 p.m. | "B" & "C" Coys. Working on Assault and Bombing Courses. |

"A" & "D" Coys as for "B" & "C" Coys on 14th August

15th Aug.

Appendix No 4.

Programme of Training and Work
16th and 17th August 1918

9th Battalion, THE MANCHESTER REGIMENT

PROGRAMME OF TRAINING

Day.	Hour.	Training and Work.

FRIDAY   8.15. - 12.30. p.m.   "A" & "B" Coys.   Working on Assault Course.
          8.30. - 11.30. a.m.   "D" Coy.   South Range.
          11.30. - 1.0. p.m.   Signllrs & Scouts   South Range.
          1.30. - 4.30. p.m.   "C" Coy   South Range.
          Coys. on range will fire bombers first and then send them to A.C.
6 Aug.   for work under bombing Officer, others Gas Training
          8.30. - 12.30. p.m.   H.Q. L.G. Section   Anti-Aircraft Course.
          8.30. - 1.30. p.m.   Junior N.C.Os.   Classes.

SATURDAY   8.15. - 12.30. p.m.   "B" & "C" Coys   Working on Assault Course.
          8.30. - 11.30. a.m.   "A" Coy.   South Range.
          11.30. - 1.0. p.m.   Signllrs & Scouts   South Range.
          1.30. - 4.30. p.m.   "D" Coy   South Range.
          Coys. on range will fire bombers first and then send them to A.C.
7 Aug.   for work under Bombing Officer, others Gas.
          8.30. - 12.30. p.m.   H.Q. L.G. Section   Anti-Aircraft Course.
          8.30. - 12.30. p.m.   Junior N.C.Os   Test.

          2. 0. p.m. Coy.   Officers and N.C.Os Scheme.

                                        AND ADJT.,
                            9th Bn. Manchester Regiment.

Major. CML Scott.

Appendix No 5

Programme of Training & Work

19th and 20th August 1918.

9th BATTALION, MANCHESTER REGIMENT.
PROGRAMME OF TRAINING AND WORK.

Hour		TRAINING & WORK
	MONDAY, 19th AUGUST 1918.	
9. 0 - 12. 0 Noon	"A" & "D" Coys	Working on Assault Course C2. Actual hours of work to be not less than 3 hours.
8.30.- 12.30 pm	"C" Coy.	Range B2.
2. 0 - 6. 0 pm	"B" Coy.	Range B2.
8.30 - 12.30 pm	HQ. LG. Section.	Anti-Aircraft Course.
8.30. -12.30.pm	Junior N.C.Os Class.	New Class.
8.30 - 12.30.pm	Officers	Bde P.T.&B.F. for Officers as detailed
	TUESDAY, 20th AUGUST 1918.	
8.30 - 12.30 pm	"D" Coy	Range B 2.
2. 0 - 6. 0 pm	"A" "	Range B 2.
9. 0 - 12. 0 Noon	"C" & "B" Coys	Working on Assault Course C2. Actual hours of work to not less than 3 hours.
8.30 - 12.30.pm	HQ. LG. Section.	Anti-Aircraft Course.
8.30 - 12.30 pm	Junior N.C.Os	New Class.
9. 0 - 12. 0 Noon	"A" Coys	Baths.
2. 0 - 5. 0 pm	"D". "	Baths.
2.30 pm	Officers & N.C.Os	GAS, Lecture in Camp.

Appendix No. 6

Programme of Training & Work.
21st and 22nd August 1918

9th Bn. MANCHESTER REGIMENT
PROGRAMME OF WORK AND TRAINING.

Hours.		Work and Training
WEDNESDAY - AUGUST 21st 1918		
9. 0. - 12. 0 Noon.	"A" & "D" Coys.	Working on Assault Course - Actual hours of work to be not less than 3 hrs
8.30. - 12.30 p.m.	"B" Coy.	North Range.
~~8.30. - 12.30.p.m.~~ 2-6 pm	"C" Coy.	North Range.
8.30. - 12.30 p.m.	Junior N.C.Os	Class.
8.30. - 12.30.p.m.	Lewis Gunners	Anti-Aircraft Course.
8.30. - 12.30.p.m.	Lewis Gunners	Beginners Class.
8.30 - 12.30.p.m.	Officers.	P. & B. T. Course - B3 Area.
8 30 - 12.30.p.m.	"C" Coy.	Baths.
9. 0. - 12. 0.Noon	"B" Coy.	Baths.
2. 0. - 5. 0. p.m.		
5.30.p.m.	Officers.	Discussion for young Officers in Schoolroom opposite Bde H.Q. All Officers below rank of Major to attend.
THURSDAY - AUGUST 22nd 1918		
9. 0. - 12. 0. Noon.	"B" & "C" Coys.	Working on Assault Course - Actual hours of work to be not less than 3 hours.
8.30. - 12.30.p.m.	"A" Coy	North Range.
8.30 - 12.30.p.m.	"D" Coy.	North Range.
8.30. - 12.30 p.m.	Junior N.C.Os	Class.
8.30. - 12.30.p.m.	Lewis Gunners	Anti-Aircraft Course.
8.30. - 12.30.p.m.	Lewis Gunners	Beginners' Course.
8.30 - 12.30 p.m.	Officers	P. & B. T. Course - B.3 Area.
2.30.p.m.		Lecture by Brigade Major on Writing Messages & Reports
5.30.p.m.		All officers to discuss Tactical Scheme No.3.

L A Turvey
CAPT. AND ADJT.
9th Battalion, Manchester Regiment.

20.8.18

Appendix No 7.

Programme of Training and Work.
23rd and 24th August 1918.

9th BATTALION, THE MANCHESTER REGIMENT
PROGRAMME OF WORK AND TRAINING

HOURS.		WORK AND TRAINING
FRIDAY – 23rd AUGUST 1918		
	"A" & "D" Coys.	Route march combined with digging Assault Course – not less than 3 hours digging.
8.30. – 12.30.p.m.	"C" Coy.	South Range.
2.0. – 6.0.p.m.	"B" "	South Range.
8.30. – 12.30.p.m.	Junior N.C.Os.	Class.
8.30. – 12.30.p.m.	Lewis Gunners	Anti-Aircraft Course
8.30. – 12.30.p.m.	Lewis Gunners	Beginners Class.
8.30. – 12.30.p.m.	Officers	Bde P.& B.T.Course – B3 Area.
SATURDAY. 24th AUGUST 1918		
7.0. – 9.30.a.m.		Battalion Route March – Full Marching Order without packs. Coys. parade behind "D" Coy lines 6.50.a.m ready to move off.
11.30.a.m.		FEET AND KIT INSPECTION – All Companies.
9.0.a.m.		Tactical Scheme for officers and N.C.Os. on ground selected near MIN de PIERRES as Battalion returns from Route March. Battalion to be marched back to camp under R.S.M. and C.S.Ms. will be in charge of Coys.

L A Turvey
CAPT. AND ADJT.,
9th Battalion, THE MANCHESTER REGIMENT

22nd Aug. 1918

Appendix no 8

Programme of Training and Work
26th Aug 1918

9th BATTALION, MANCHESTER REGIMENT
PROGRAMME OF WORK AND TRAINING

MONDAY, - 26.8.18.

8.a.m. -	"B" &	C.2.	Route march combined with digging on
1.p.m.	"C" Coys.		Bombing Course and pits.
2.0.p.m.	do	In Camp	Quinine parade and Recreational Training.
8 - 9 am.	"A" & "D"	In Camp.	R.S.M's parade.
9.30-11.am	"A" Coy.	B.3.	Bayonet Training, with and without Gas Masks) on Assault Course.
11.30-12.30	"A"	In Camp	Musketry
2.p.m.	"A" Coy.	do	Quinine Parade and Recreational Training.
2.15-4.15pm	"A"		Baths.
9.30-10.30	"D" Coy.	In Camp	Coy. Inspection and Musketry
10.45-12.30	"D"	B.3	Bayonet Training on Assault Course, with and without Gas Masks.
2.p.m.	"D"		Quinine Parade and Recreational Training.
4.30-6.30 pm	"D"		Baths.
9.30-12.30pm	Specialists In Training Camp		Scouts Training, Lewis Gun Beginners' Class. Signallers Class.
2.p.m.	do		Quinine Parade and recreational training.
8.30-12.30	Anti-Air Craft LG Training	In Camp.	Commencement of New Class.
2.30.p.m.	do		Old Class - Firing.

N.B. ALL SPECIALISTS, except New Anti Aircraft L.G.Class, will attend R.S.M's parade.

MAJOR
for Capt. and Adjt.,
9th Bn. Manchester Regiment

Appendix no 9

Programme of Training and Work
27th August 1918

9th BATTALION, MANCHESTER REGIMENT.

PROGRAMME OF WORK AND TRAINING — TUESDAY, AUGUST 27, 1918

Time	Unit	Location	Activity
8.a.m.–1.pm.	"A" & "D"	C.2.	Route march combined with digging on bombing pits.
2.p.m.	do	In Camp	Quinine Parade and Recreational Training
8.–9.a.m.	"B" & "C"	In Camp	R.S.Ms parade.
10.–12.30pm	"B"	North Range	Application practices and gas drill.
2.p.m.	"B"	In Camp	Quinine Parade and Recreational Training
1.45.p.m.	"C"	In Camp.	Quinine Parade.
2.30–4.30.p.m.	"C"	North Range	Individual practices and gas drill.
8.30–12.30pm	Anti Aircraft L.G. Class.	In Camp.	Training.
9.30–12.30pm	Specialists	In Camp.	Lewis Gunners, Scouts, Signallers and Junior N.C.Os Class – Training.
2.30.p.m.	LECTURE.	In Camp	Tactical handling of L.Gs and V.Gs.

N.B. ALL SPECIALISTS except L.G. ~~and anti~~ anti-air class will attend R.S.Ms parade.

L.A. Tivey
CAPT. AND ADJT.,
9th Battn. Manchester Regiment.

CONFIDENTIAL.

WAR DIARY.

OF

9th Bn MANCHESTER REGT.

From 1st to 30th SEPTEMBER 1915

VOLUME No 4 — No 9.

Army Form C. 2118.

WAR DIARY
INTELLIGENCE SUMMARY

Army Form C. 2118.

(Erase heading not required.)

O.C. 2/6 Bn. The Manchester Regt.

September 1918.

Place	Date	Hour	Summary of Events and Information	Remarks and references to Appendices
HAUDRECOURT	1-9-18		Church Services as usual and baths. Programme of Training (Appendix No 1.) for week ending 7-9-18 issued.	Ref Maps FRANCE DIEPPE 16 1:100,000 Appendix No 1
-do-	2-9-18		Training as per programme (Appendix No 1.). 1 OR struck off effective strength on admission to hosp'tl whilst on leave. Left unit to effect from 20-8-15. 2 OR proceeded to "H" I.B.D. and are struck off effective strength in accordance with D.R.O. Circular Public No 24 dt 10-7-15, with effect from 2-9-18. 4 OR are struck off effective strength 2-9-18 on proceeding to "H" I.B.D.	
-do-	3-9-18		Training as per programme. The G.O.C. ordered Battalions to carry out platoon competitions and Battalions will produce 2 platoons for the Brigade Competition. On the 24th inst the Brigade platoon training (marching order) (a) Drill, close order Handling arms. (b) 23rd inst: Platoon competitions and Asslt. Course Physical Training. (c) Field practices at full ammunition. (d) Tactical handling scheme. Strength of platoon to be made up as follows: Platoon H.Q. 1 Sgt, 1 Batman, 1 Runner, 1 Platoon Sergt; Lewis Gun Section 11; 2 Rifle Sections of 7 each, 14. Total 29. 7 OR having joined the Battalion and taken on the effective strength 3-9-18. 2 Lieut S.H. HODGES, 'A' Coy and R.O. 3678 Pte Lobb, 'D' Coy, are rendered to UK 18-9-15 and are struck off the strength of the Bn from that date under K.R.O. 10 OR are struck off effective strength from various dates on admission to hospital in UK, whilst on leave. 1 OR having reported is again taken on strength from 2-9-18. 3 OR are struck off effective strength from various dates after 7 days in hospital.	
-do-	4-9-18		Training per programme. T.A.B. inoculation. The G.O.C. has laid down the minimum number men per Battalion to be fully trained in the use of the Lewis Gun as 146, the necessary number of men to be put into Training forthwith. 3 OR are struck off the effective strength of the Bn on admission to various hospitals whilst on leave in U.K. from various dates.	
-do-	5-9-18		Training per programme. The numbers of rifle grenadiers of A.LI. strength of 1 Platoon will vary according to the strength of the Battalion. Minimum strength 6, maximum strength 10.	
-d-	6-9-18		Training per programme. 3 O.R. having rejoined are again taken on the effective strength from 6-9-18, and 1 OR as above from 2-9-18. 29 OR reinforcements having joined the Battalion, are taken on from 6-9-18.	

D. D. & L., London, E.C.
(A8001) Wt. W1771/M2931 750,000 5/17 Sch. 52 Forms/C2118/14

Army Form C. 2118.

WAR DIARY

INTELLIGENCE SUMMARY.

(Erase heading not required.)

September 1918 9/7 Bn The Manchester Regt.

Place	Date	Hour	Summary of Events and Information	Remarks and references to Appendices
HAUDRICOURT	7-9-18		Training as per programme. (Appendix No.) Programme of Training for Week ending 14-9-18 received (Appendix No.2). The following events of the Brigade meeting will take place on the dates shown - Cross Country Run 14-9-18. Rifle meeting 13-9-18. Brigade Sports 21-9-18. Transport Sports 22-9-18. Football Final 24-9-18. 1 O.R. struck off effective strength 20-8-18 whilst on leave. 1 O.R. is compulsorily transferred from 2nd/7th Batt. Manchester Regt 6-8-18. Extract from LONDON GAZETTE No 30848 d/16-9-18. No 377735 Cpl A UNSWORTH DCM awarded Military Military.	FRANCE DIEPPE 1/10,000 September 1918
-do-	8-9-18		Church Services. Parade Services for Brigade aboard. On issue of instructions of the Medical Officer to men undergoing Out-Patient Treatment will be made twice weekly at Training Ground. 1 O.R. is struck off effective strength on evacuation to Stationary hospital Rouen 5-4-18. Route for Cross Country Run:- Across country to VILLERS-ROUPIED RD — RD to LOZIERES — N.E. along HAUDRICOURT-AUMALE RD, South along road towards LANNOY-GUILLIERE, - S.W. to A2 area crossing of A1 area and road, cross steep spur, miniature range across HAUDRICOURT-AUMALE RD. Finishing point — Sports Ground.	
-do-	9-9-18		Training as per programme. 15 OR having joined the Battalion are taken on the effective strength from 9-9-15. No 5098 Pte W. TOMKINSON died in hospital 4-9-18.	
-do-	10-9-18		Training as per programme. Following lectures will take place – "Attack in mobile warfare" by G.O.C. 10-9-18. "History of American Army" by special lecturer 11-9-18. 5 OR are struck off effective strength on admission to hospital in U.K. whilst on leave, from various dates. "Marching issues" by Col. CHARTRIS 12-9-18.	
-do-	11-9-18		Training as per programme. Rifle Platoon Training. There are now only three sections and platoon, one of which is a double Lewis Gun Section, and the remaining two may if effective (1 N.C.O. and 10 men) 2 Rifle Sections (N.C.O. and 10 men) (always excepting) 1 L.G. Section of (1 N.C.O. + 6 men) 3 men of each of these rifle sections to be trained as Rifle Grenadiers. (Total 29.) All men up to this 29 will be refund to as reserves. 6 O.R. struck off effective strength after 4 days in hospital with effect from various dates.	

Army Form C. 2118.

WAR DIARY
INTELLIGENCE SUMMARY
(Erase heading not required.)

Title pages September 1918

9th Bn The Manchester Regt

Place	Date	Hour	Summary of Events and Information	Remarks and references to Appendices
HAUDRICOURT	12-9-18		Training as per programme. Following receipt from Headquarters 66th Division M.S. to C in C 6306. 6th Dec 6683/1/A with reference to the attached. The 9th Bn MANCHESTER REGT, and the 6th Bn LANCASHIRE FUSILIERS are Territorial Battalions, and the 13th Bn MANCHESTER REGT, and 12th Bn LANCASHIRE FUSILIERS have ceased to exist. (Sd) --- Lt Col A.M.S. for Major General Military Secretary to Commander-in-chief. G.A.Q. 3-9-18.	Ref maps FRANCE DIEPPE 16 1:100,000
-do-	13-9-18		Training as per programme. 1 O.R. so struck off the effective strength of the Battalion on admission to hospital in U.K. 4-9-18. 10 R. having rejoined as taken on the strength 12-9-18. 18 O.R. are struck off the effective strength on being absorbed into the authorised establishment of the 199th L.T.M.B.	Appendix No 3
-do-	14-9-18		Training as per programme. Programme of Training, week ending 21-9-18 (Appendix No 3) issued. 1 O.R. struck off the effective strength on admission to hospital BOULOGNE 11-9-18. 1 O.R. having rejoined is taken on strength 13-9-18.	Appendix No 3
-do-	15-9-18		Church Service as usual. Result of Cross Country Run. 1st 5/6 CONNAUGHT RANGERS 166767 points. 2nd 6th Bn LANCASHIRE FUSILIERS 74 283 points. Points for Brigade Championship. 9th MANCHESTER REGT 124329 points 3rd 6th Bn LANCASHIRE FUSILIERS 10 points, 9th MANCHESTER REGT 4 points. will be counted as under: 5/6th CONNAUGHT RANGERS 10 points, 9th MANCHESTER REGT 4 points.	
-do-	16-9-18		Training as per programme (Appendix No 3) 3 O.R. having rejoined are taken on effective strength 15-9-18. Lieut J A SPURLING A.Cy having proceeded to base in abord once with 199th Bde A 806 dd 15-9-18, is struck off the effective strength of the Battalion, 16-9-18. 1 O.R. struck off effective strength on evacuation to stationary hospital ABANCOURT 15-9-18, and 1 O.R. on admission to Civil Hospital WIGAN whilst on leave 29-7-18	
-do- -do-	17-9-15 18-9-18		Training as per programme. Training as per programme. T.A.B. inoculation. Extract from LONDON GAZETTE dt 3-9-18. No 11760. 30 R. Sgt W. BROOKS, D.C.M. awarded M.S.M. 2 O.R. are struck off effective strength after 7 days in hospital 9-9-15. 30 O.R. having rejoined are again taken on 17-9-15. 1 O.R. is struck off effective strength on admission to hospital MANCHESTER 9-9-15. Battalion Sports.	

Army Form C. 2118.

WAR DIARY
or
INTELLIGENCE SUMMARY.
(Erase heading not required.)

Title pages September 1918.

Army 9th Bn. Manchester Regt.

Instructions regarding War Diaries and Intelligence Summaries are contained in F.S. Regs., Part II. and the Staff Manual respectively. Title pages will be prepared in manuscript.

Place	Date	Hour	Summary of Events and Information	Remarks and references to Appendices
HAUDRICOURT	19-9-18		Training cancelled. Operation Order No 1 issued (Appendix No 4) The Battalion will move from L.of C. area to 1st Army area. Tomorrow 20th inst, and will march to FORMERIE Station to entrain. T.O.R. on strength after effecting strength on entrainment to hospital ROUEN 17-9-18. 5 O.R. are struck off effective. strength after 7 days in hospital from various units.	Ref. Maps. FRANCE. DIEPPE 16 LENS Bn 2. 11. 1/100,000. Appendix No 4
-do-	20-9-18		Battalion marched to FORMERIE and entrained. Train left at 7pm. Entraining state, 29 Officers 463 O.R. 17 Vehicles, 53 animals.	
PENIN	21-9-18		Battalion arrived PENIN 6 am after detraining at TINQUES. Battalion rested in billets. 3 O.R. missing reported are taken on from 19-9-18. Operation Order No 2 (Appendix No 5) issued. The Battalion marched to MANIN, billets were taken over from 6th LANCS. FUS. 9th GLOUCESTER REGT took over Battalion billets at PENIN. Capt ? DARLINGTON & ? returned from leave to U.K.	Appendix No 5
-do- MANIN	22-9-18			
-do-	23-9-18		Training consisting of organising coys into platoons of 4 platoons each, and practice in attack formation. The boundary of the Battn billets ?are north limits of the village. The 64 LANCS FUS have now joined the 148 Brigade and the 18th ?????(LANCS. HUSSARS. YEOMANRY) Kings LIVERPOOL REGT has now joined the 199th INF. BDE. Brigade H.Q. are at IZEL-LES-HAMEAU. and 66th DIV at LE CAUROY. 5/ CONNAUGHT RANGERS are at IZEL-near Bde H.Q. and 18th LIVERPOOL REGT at GIVENCHY-LE-NOBLE. ??? Divisional Commander has decided that a pack will be carried and not a haversack. (?Battle Order. ?Therefore will consist as under: - Steel helmet Box Respirator, 150 rounds in pouches (U.S.E.) or 120 rounds in remainder (Rifles). Entrenching tool (left behind if spade is carried) Tools, Toggle Soar. Holdall (complete) oil can, 1½ pairs 2 days rations (including iron rations). 1 m? cards, 20 rounds S.A.A. (in pocket U.S.E.) 60 in ???? S.A.A. (in pouch if latter) Oilskin. Any extra ammunition to be carried in bandoliers. When grenades are carried (or present at disposition of C.O) 6 rifle grenades and 105 rounds S.A.A. to be carried by bomber per 6 ???? system. T.O.R. Lewis Gun school are struck off effective ?????? strength 3-?-8 and limits to U.R. with effects from 12-9-18. L/C ??? sent to ?????????? to Depot from 12-9-18. 3 O.R. "N" School in still the effective strength ?????????? ???????? effects from 21-9-18.	
-do-	24-9-18		Enemy planes passed over at about 9.00 am and dropped hundreds of ?????lls (Appendix No 6) they covered HAUDRICOURT a large area of country around the village.	Appendix No 6

Army Form C. 2118.

WAR DIARY
INTELLIGENCE SUMMARY.
(Erase heading not required.)

9th Bn Manchester Regt

September 1918

Instructions regarding War Diaries and Intelligence Summaries are contained in F.S. Regs., Part II. and the Staff Manual respectively. Title pages will be prepared in manuscript.

Place	Date	Hour	Summary of Events and Information	Remarks and references to Appendices
MANIN	24-9-18 (contd)		All companies practised the attack in the forenoon. In the afternoon, Adjutant and Coy Commanders assembled at Brigade H.Q. and afterwards practised the ground the Brigade scheme which will take place on the 26th inst. 4 O.R. are struck off the effective strength after 4 days in hospital 24-9-18.	Adjt Lt R. Leigh FRANCE LENS Qu 2. 11. AMIENS 17.
-do-	25-9-18		Brigade Route march. All men in marching order, and all transport loaded and present. Length of route about 11 miles.	Appendix 1
-do-	26-9-18		Brigade Scheme carried out according to scheme attached (Appendix No 2). 2/Lieut F.RUDDY, MC DCM and 2/Lieut D.HAMILTON are struck off the strength of the Battalion with effect from 4/5-9-18 on being posted to 199th L.T.M.B. Authority, A.G./2158/5239. 3 O.R. are struck off effective strength after 4 days in hospital 25-9-18. 1 O.R. Leaving rejoined from hospital is again taken on 25-9-18.	Appendix No 2
-do-	27-9-18		Battalion paraded for Brigade Route march. Operation Order No 3 (Appendix No 8) issued.	Appendix No 3
-do-	28-9-18		Battalion entrained at TINQUES and moved via ARRAS and ALBERT to CORBIE where it billeted for the night. Capt. G.T. NEWMAN proceeded on leave to U.K. Operation Order No 4 (Appendix No 9) issued.	Appendix No 4
-do-	29-9-18		Battalion moved to PROYART.	
-do-	30-9-18		Battalion received Operation Order No 5 issued (Appendix No 10). The Battalion will proceed to MARICOURT tomorrow. They contacted 24 hours clock system will be adopted throughout the British Army from midnight 30th Sept 1918. The effective strength of the Battalion is 31 Officers and 754 other ranks.	Appendix No 5

1-10-18

Lieut Col
9th Bn Manchester Regt

Appendix No 1.

Programme of Training – week ending 7-9-18

9th BN. MANCHESTER REGIMENT.

PROGRAMME OF TRAINING - week ending 7/9/18.

DAY.	HOURS.	AREA.	TRAINING.	REMARKS.
	7.30 - 8.00.	Camp.	P.T. for all Coys, Band & Specialists, also Battn Footballers under 2/Lt Fazackerley.	
	8.15 -10.15.	B.2.	"C" Coy. Practices 1, 2, & 3 Musketry Course for all men not fired.	
	10.15 -12.00.	"	"D" Coy. do. do.	
	8.15 - 9.15.	Camp.	A, B, & D Coys. Coy Drill & Handling of Arms.	
	9.30 -10.00.	"	A & B Coys. Musketry Instruction.	
	10.15 -10.45.	"	A & B Coys. Gas Drill.	
MONDAY.	11.00 -12.00.	"	C. Coy., Coy Drill & Handling of Arms.	
	1.30 p.m.		Quinine Parade.	
2nd SEPT.	2.00 - 4.00.	B.2.	"A" Coy. Firing practices 1, 2, & 3 Musketry Course. All men not already fired.	
	4.30 - 6.30.	"	"B" Coy. do. do.	
	2.00 p.m.	Camp.	"C" & "D" Coys. Lecture by M.O.	
	9.30 -12.00.	"	Specialists Training, i.e. Coy L.G. classes, Scouts & L.G. Scouts under Scout Off., Junior N.C.Os class - Exam. by O.C.	
	7.30 a.m.		Battn Route March with Battn Drill en route, & Route March back to camp. Dress, Marching Order with Packs.	
	11.30 "	Camp.	Foot and Rifle Inspection.	
TUESDAY.	1.30 p.m.	"	Quinine Parade.	
	2.00 - 4.00.	B.2.	Musketry, Practices 1, 2 & 3 of Course for H.Qrs (Transport, Runners, Lewis Gunners & Q.M. Stores) under Transport Officer.	
3rd SEPT.				
	4.30 - 5.30.	B.2.	do. for Band, under Orderly Off.	
	6.00 - 6.45.	Camp.	Lecture & discussion by O.C.C. for all Officers on "Task Work".	
	3.00.		Officers Riding Class.	
			Recreational Training.	
	7.30 - 8.15.	Camp.	A & B Coys & Specialists (i.e. Bandsmen, Bn. Footballers, & Coy. L.G. Classes) P.T.,	
	9.00 -10.00	"	Bayonet Training.	
	10.15 -10.45.	"	Musketry Instruction.	
	7.30 - 9.30.	C.1.	"C" Coy. Route March to Area. Grenade training, Drill, & Handling of Arms.	
WEDNESDAY.		C.2.	"D" Coy. Route March to Area. Bombing (live bombs) & Bayonet Training on Assault Course.	
4th SEPT.	10.00 -11.30.	C.1.	"D" Coy. as for "C" Coy. above.	
		C.2.	"C" " " " "D" " "	
	8.30 -12.30.	Camp.	Specialist training. Coy L.G. Classes, Scouts & L.G. Scouts Class.	
	1.30 p.m.		Quinine Parade.	
	2.00 - 4.00	North Range.	"B" Coy. Practices 4 & 5, and 300 yds practice No. 7, for all men not fired.	
	4.00 - 6.00	"	"A" Coy. do. do.	
	6.00 p.m.	Camp.	Lecture by G.S.O. 2 to all Officers & N.C.Os. on "Machine Guns".	
	3 p.m. onwards.		Recreational Training.	
		N.B.,	North Range available for Scouts all the morning.	

DAY.	HOURS.	AREA.	TRAINING.	REMARKS.

P.T.O.

DAY.	HOURS.	AREA.	WORK.	REMARKS.
THURSDAY. 5th SEPT.	AS FOR WEDNESDAY. 3 p.m. onwards.	do.	"A" & "B" Coys as for "C" & "D". "C" & "D" " " " "A" & "B". Specialists as for Wednesday. Recreational Training. N.B., North Range available for Scouts all morning.	
FRIDAY. 6th SEPT.	7.30 – 8.30. 8.30 –11.30.	Camp. A.1. A.2.	Adjutant's Parade. All Specialists to attend. "B" Coy. Completion of Individual Musketry Course on South Range. (200 yds & 300 yds). C. & D. Coys. Bombing, Rifle Grenade training, and tactical handling of L.Gs.	
	9.00 –10.00. 8.30 –12.00. 1.30 p.m. 2.00 – 5.00. 2.30 p.m. 3.00 " 6.00 "	Camp. " A.1.	"A" Coy. Half, Musketry Instruction. Half, Gas Drill. Specialists Training, i.e. Coy L.G. Class, Scouts & L.G. Scouts. Quinine Parade. "A" Coy. Completion of Individual Musketry Course on South Range. (200 yds & 300 yds). Officers Discussion at School opposite Brigade Headquarters. Officers Riding School. Lecture by Staff Captain to all Off. & N.C.Os. on "Supply of Ammun. in the Field". Recreational Training.	
SATURDAY. 7th SEPT.	7.30 – 8.15. As for FRIDAY.	Camp. As for FRI.	P.T. for all Coys. & Specialists. A & B Coys, as for C. & D. Coys above. C & D " " " " A & B " " Specialists as for Friday.	
SUNDAY. 8th SEPT.	2.00 p.m.	Camp. Camp. "	Tactical Scheme for A, B, & D Coy Officers. Parade Service for all Denominations. Striking of Tents & scrubbing tent boards, and Domestic fatigues. Rifle Meeting.	

DAILY BAND PROGRAMME.

	7.30 – 8.15.	Camp.	P.T.)	
	9.00 –11.00	"	Band Practice.)	
	11.30 –12.00	"	Gas Drill)	under A/R.S.M.
	2.00 – 3.00	"	Band Practice.)	HARRISON.
	5.00 – 6.00	"	Voluntary Band Practice.)	

N.B., Band will attend Adjutant's parades.

NOTES :-   Trained Lewis Gunners fire with Company.
Times given in programme are the hours training commences and ends, so extra time must be allowed for getting to and from Area.
All Musketry Practices will be carried out in Steel Helmets.
Bombs and Grenades will always be taken to training Area by Companies when bombing and rifle grenading takes place.

L. A. Turvey
Captain & Adjutant.
for Lieut. Colonel.
Comdg. 8th Bn. Manchester Regiment.

1/9/18.

APPENDIX No 2.

PROGRAMME of TRAINING week ending 14-9-18.

9th BN. MANCHESTER REGIMENT.
PROGRAMME OF TRAINING - week ending 14/9/18.

DAY.	HOURS.	AREA.	WORK & TRAINING.	REMARKS.
MONDAY, 9th Sept.	7.30 a.m.		"A" & "B" Coys. Route March. Dress - Marching Order. Full Packs. Trained Specialists to parade. Route - Camp, ROUPIED, BARQUES, ILLOIS, COUPIGNE, HAUDRICOURT. Foot & Rifle inspection on return to Camp.	
	8.00 - 12.00. a.m.	B.2.	All Coys. L.G. Classes firing on Short Range, & training.	
	8.00 - 12.00. a.m.	B.3.	"C" & "D" Coys. 2 hours each Bayonet training on Assault Course under Army Gymnastic Instructor Sgt. Myles. Remaining 2 hours - 1 hour Drill, ½ hr Gas, ½ hr Fire control and recognition of targets.	
	8.00 - 12.00. a.m.		L.G. Scouts under Scout Officer. A.A. Class under B.L.G. Officer.	
	1.30 p.m.		Quinine Parade.	
	2.00 - 4.00. p.m.	B.2.	"H.Q." Coy. firing on Short Range under Orderly Officer.	
	4.30 - 6.30.	"	"A" & "B" Coys. 3rd Class Shots on Short Range.	
	2.00 p.m.		"C" & "D" Coys. Cross County Run, Training.	
			All Coys. training for Sports.	
TUESDAY, 10th Sept.	As for Monday.	As for Monday.	"A" & "B" Coys as for "C" & "D" Coys. on Monday throughout & vice versa.	
	6.00 p.m.	Camp.	Lecture by G.O.C. "Tactics in Mobile Warfare".	
	2.00 p.m.		Training for Cross Country Run and Sports.	
	Evening.		Semi-final, Bde Football Comp. Battalion V A.S.C.	
WEDNESDAY, 11th Sept.	8.00 -12.00 a.m.	C.1.	"A" & "B" Coys. Platoon training in the attack, with L.Gs, R.Gs, etc (Platoons to be made up to strength & classes taken on parade), and carrying out of Tactical Ex.	
	" "	A.1.	"D" Coy. Elementary Platoon Field Practices, with L.Gs, on "A" Range. (L.G. Classes to be taken & platoons made up to strength).	
	" "	C.2.	"C" Coy. Bombing and R.G. Training, and use of Entrenching Tool.	
	" "	Camp.	L.G. Scouts under Scout Officer. A.A. Class under B.L.G.O.	
	1.30 p.m.		Quinine Parade.	
	All afternoon.	A.1.	Company Rifle Teams practice on "A" Range.	
	2.00 - 3.00.	Camp.	Coy. 3rd Class Shots. Musketry Instrn.	
	2.00 p.m. onwards.		Coys. training for Cross Country Run & Sports. Tug-o-War etc.	
	3.00 p.m.		Officers Riding Class.	
THURSDAY, 12th Sept.	8.00 -12.00.	C.1.	"C" & "D" Coys as for "A" & "B" above.	
	" "	A.1.	"A" Coy. as for "D" Coy. above.	
	" "	C.2.	"B" " " " "C" " "	
			L.G. Scouts & A.A. Class as for Wednesday.	
	1.30 p.m.		Quinine Parade.	
	afternoon.	A.1.& Camp.	As for Wednesday.	
	2 p.m. onwards.		Coys. training for Cross Country Run & Sports. Tug-o-War etc.	

P.T.O.

DAY.	HOURS.	AREA.	WORK & TRAINING.	REMARKS.
FRIDAY. 13th Sept.	7.30 – 8.15. a.m.	Camp.	C.O's Ceremonial Parade. (strong as possible).	
	9.00 –12.00.	A.1.	"B" Coy. Elementary Platoon Field Practice (L.G. Classes to attend & Platoons to be made up to strength) B. Range.	
	" "	A.2.	"A","C",& "D" Coys. R.G. training, Use of Entrenching Tool & L.G. tactical handling.	
	" "		L.G. Scouts & A.A. L.Grs. under Scout Officer & B.L.G.O. Training.	
	afternoon.		Lecture by on "Machine Guns.	
	1.30 p.m.		Brigade Rifle Meeting on A,B,& C ranges.	
SATURDAY, 14th Sept.	7.30 – 8.15.	Camp.	P.T., All Specialists to attend.	
	9.00 –12.00.	A.1.	"C" Coy. as for "B" Coy. above.	
	" "	A.2.	"A","B",& "D" Coys. as for "A","C", & "D" Coys above.	
			L.G. Scouts & A.A. Class as for Friday.	
	Afternoon.		Brigade Inter-battalion Cross Country Run. Recreational training.	
SUNDAY. 15th Sept.	Morning.		Voluntary Church Service. Striking of Tents & scrubbing of tent boards. Domestic Fatigues,i.e. Ironing & washing clothing, and Kit Inspn.	
	Afternoon.		Recreation.	
			BAND PROGRAMME of Training as for last week. They will attend C.O's parade.	

NOTES :-   Trained Lewis Gunners fire with Company.
Times given in programme are the hours training commences and ends, so extra time must be allowed for getting to and from Area.
All Musketry Practices will be carried out in Steel Helmets.
Bombs and Grenades will always be taken to training Area by Companies when bombing and rifle grenading takes place.

L A Turvey

Captain & Adjutant.
for Lieut. Colonel.
Comdg. 9th Bn. Manchester Regt.

7/9/18.

APPENDIX No 3.

PROGRAMME OF TRAINING — week ending 21-9-18.

9th BN. MANCHESTER REGIMENT.

PROGRAMME OF TRAINING – week ending 21/9/18.

DAY.	HOURS.	Coy.	AREA.	REMARKS.
MONDAY, 16th Septr.	7.45 a.m.	ALL.	Camp.	Coys. Inspection.
	8.30/12.30.	A & B.	A.1.	"A" Coy. Firing Platoon Field Practices, & completing 500 yds Appln. on "A" range for whole Company.
				"B" Coy. Firing Platoon Field Practices, & compltg. 500 yds Appln. with whole Coy, on "C" range. Intervening ground to be used for manoeuvring of L.Gs. during Field Practices according to scheme.
	8.30/12.00.	"D"	Camp.	Company on Duty Training in camp, & Gas Drill, 3rd Class Shots etc.
	10.30.	"C"	do.	Musketry Instruction & ½ hr Gas Drill. Battn. & Coy. employ ¼ hr Gas Drill under Orderly Officer.
	1.30/5.30.	"C"	A.1.	Firing Platoon Field Practices & compltg. 500 yds Appln. with whole Coy, on "C" range.
	" "	"H.Q"	"	Firing Practices at 200 yds & 300 yds on "A" range under Lt. Allen & 2/Lt. Groves.
	1.30 p.m.	Camp.(ALL).		Quinine Parade.
	3.00 "			Officers' Riding School.
				Training for Battn. & Brigade Sports.
TUESDAY 17th Septr.	7.45 a.m.	ALL.	Camp.	Coys. Inspection.
	8.30/11.30.	B & C.,	A2.	Rifle Grenade Training, tactical handling of L.Gs. and Gas Drill.
	do.	"D"	A1.	Firing Platoon Field Practices & completion of 500 yds Appln. with whole Coy. on "C" range.
	do.	B & C. (casuals)	"	Firing practices at 200 yds & 300 yds on "A" range. Officers for superintending will be published in Battn. Orders.
	do.	"A"	Camp.	Company on Duty. Training, 3rd Class Shots etc.
	10.30 a.m.		"	Battn & Coy. Employ. ¼ hr Gas Drill under Orderly Officer.
	1.00/6.30p.m.	ALL.	A1.	Brigade Rifle Meeting. (Training for Battn & Brigade Sports.)
	6.30. "	"	Camp.	Quinine Parade.
WEDNESDAY. 18th Septr.	7.45 a.m.	ALL.	Camp.	Coys. Inspection.
	8.30/11.00.	A & C.	C1.	Platoon Training according to Coy. schemes.
	" "	"D"	C2.	Bayonet & Grenade training. L.G., & Gas.
	" "	"B"	Camp.	Company on duty. Training, 3rd C. Shots etc.
	10.30a.m.		"	Battn & Coy employ. ¼ hr Gas trng. under O.Off.
	1.30pm.	ALL.	"	Quinine Parade.
	2.00pm.	"	Sports Ground.	Battalion Eliminating Sports.
				Baths for half Battalion.
THURSDAY. 19th Septr.	7.45 a.m.	ALL.	Camp.	Coys. Inspection.
	8.30/12.15.	B & D.	C1.	Platoon training according to Coy. schemes.
	" "	"A"	C2.	Bayonet & Grenade Trng., L.G., & Gas.
	" "	"C"	Camp.	Company on duty. Training 3rd Cl. shots, etc.
	10.30a.m.		"	"H.Q"., Battn. & Coy. Employ., ¼ hr Gas training under Orderly Officer.
	1.30p.m.	ALL.	"	Quinine Parade.
				Baths for half Battalion.
	2.00 " onwards.			Training for Brigade Sports.
FRIDAY. 20th Septr.	7.45 a.m.	ALL.	Camp.	Coys. Inspection.
	8.30/12.15.	"A"	B1.	Platoon training according to Coy. schemes.
	" "	B & C.	B3.	Bayonet training on Assault Course (Sgt MYLES) and platoon training.
	" "	"D"	Camp.	Company on duty. Training, Gas, 3rd Class Shots etc.
	8.30/12.15.	ALL.	B2.	Coy. L. Gunners firing on short range.
	10.30 a.m.		Camp.	"H.Q.", Battn & Coy. Employ. ¼ hr Gas Drill.

P.TO.

DAY.	HOURS.	COY.	AREA.	TRAINING.	REMARKS.
FRIDAY. 20th Sept. (Contd).	3.00 p.m. 1.30 p.m. 2.00/5. "	ALL. "	Camp. " B2.	Officers' Riding School. Quinine Parade. All Coy. 3rd Class Shots firing on Short Range under 1 Officer per Coy. 4 Targets allotted to each Coy.	
SATURDAY. 21st Septr.	7.45 a.m. 9.00 " 10.00/12.30. 1.30 pm. 2.00/6.p.m.	ALL. " " " "	Camp. " Sports) Ground) Camp. Sports) Ground)	Coys. Inspection. Commanding Officer's Inspection of Coys. & lines. Brigade Sports. Quinine Parade. Brigade Sports.	
SUNDAY. 22nd Septr.	morning. 10. a.m. 2.00 p.m.	ALL. " "		Voluntary Church Parade. Domestic Fatigues. Striking tents & scrubbing tent boards. Brigade Transport Sports. do. (The Band will play at Sports in afternoon).	

BAND PROGRAMME.

ALL WEEK.	7.45 a.m. 9/11 " 11.30 - 12.15 a.m. 1.30 p.m. 2/3.00 p.m. 5/6.00 "		Camp. " " " " "	Attend Coy. Inspection. Practice. Training in Gas, & P.T. under A/R.S.M. Quinine Parade. Practice. Voluntary Practice.	

L A Turvey

Captain & Adjutant.
for Lieut. Colonel.
Comdg. 9th Bn. Manchester Regt.

14/9/18.

Appendix No 4.

Operation Order No 1.

SECRET   Operation Order No 1   Copy No 2
                                    by
                    Lieut-Colonel J. F. B. Morrell. M.V.O.
                  Commanding 2nd Battalion, The Manchester Regiment.
Reference Map. DIEPPE. 16. 1/100,000.

1. The Battalion will move from L. of. C Area to 1st Army Area to-morrow, 20th inst, (and will march to FORMERIE Station to Entrain.) Distance of March about 10 miles.

2. Routine to-morrow
                        Reveille.   6.30. a.m.
                        Breakfast.   8. 0. a.m.
            Dinner (for Leading Party)   11.30. a.m.
               (" Battalion   )   12.0. Noon.
                        Tea   On Arrival at FORMERIE.

3. The Battalion will parade on "E" Side of Camp at 2. p.m.. Coys parade at 1.45. p.m.

4. The order on the March will be . H.Q., "D","C", Band,"B","A". Coys. Dress F.S.M.O. Steel helmets. Capes or Ground Sheets on Packs. Water bottles filled. Caps to be worn. Dismounted. Officers will wear F.S.M.O.
   Band and Drummers will parade in equipment with Instruments. One man of Band to be detailed to take charge of Packs & Rifles which will be carried on G.S. Wagon.

5. The following mobilization equipment will be carried on the March by the men responsible:— Wire Cutters, Band Saws, Field Glasses, Compasses, Grenade Discharger Cups, Rifle Chamber Cleaning Rods,—Bars & Stroud Range Finders. Remainder of Coys Mobilization Equipment Should be Sent to Q.M. Stores for Conveyance by G.S. Wagon.
   Stretchers will be Carried by S.B.s. The Packs belonging to those men being Conveyed by "Mattere Cart".

6. The Coys Field Kitchens will move with 1st Line Transport & Carry Coy mess Boxes with them. Two Cooks only, per Coy dressed in Drill Overalls with Puttees, will march with the Kitchens. Cooks Rifles & equipment must be Carried on front half of Kitchen.

7. Marching Out States are required at B.O.R. from all Coys, Transport and H.Q. 1 hour before parade at Present Camp.
   Marching in State will be Sent to B.O.R. ½ hour after Arrival in New Camp.
                                        P.T.O.

8. Rations for to-morrow 20th inst have been issued to Coys to-day. Rations for 21st and 22nd inst will be issued on arrival at destination.

9. A Loading Party consisting of 1. N.C.O. (full rank) and 10. O.Ranks from each Coy, including H.Q. will parade under 2nd Lieut. D.H.H. Davies "D" Coy & march off at 12 Mid-day to-morrow for FORMERIE Stn. to load Transport Vehicles and Baggage in the train. Party from H.Q. will include 2 Pioneers.

10. 1st and 2nd Line Transport is to be packed strictly in accordance with G.H.Q. Memo. O.B./2246 & Battalion Standing Order No 2 which have been issued previously.
 Transport will move off at 1. p.m. under Transport Officer.

11. The Camp is to be left scrupulously clean & tent curtains rolled up. The Battalion Orderly Officer will inspect Camp, including Transport Lines, before the Battalion moves off.
 All Marquees & Tents are to be left Standing.

L. A. Turvey.

Captain & Adjutant.
9th Battalion, The Manchester Regiment.

Issued at 10 p.m.
 Distribution:—
No 1. Commanding Officer.
 2} War Diary.
 3}
 4 Major Scott.
 5 O.C. A. Coy
 6   " B "
 7   " C "
 8   " D "
 9   " H.Q.
 10 Medical Officer.
 11 Signal
 12 Transport.
 13 Q.M.
 14 File.

Appendix No 6

Operation Order No 2

SECRET.   Copy No. 8

OPERATION ORDER NO. 2.

By Lt-Col. J. F. B. Morrell, M.V.O., Commanding
9th Battalion Manchester Regt.

Ref. MAP LENS 11, Edition 2.

1. The Battn. will move this afternoon to MANIN. Move to be completed by 5 p.m.

2. The order for the march will be as follows. Band and Drums. HQ. Coy. C. A. B. D Coys. C Coy to reach HQ. by 2.15 p.m.

3. 2/Lt. EGAN and C.Q.M.S.s, or a Sergt., from each Coy. and HQ. will proceed at 9.30 a.m. on bicycles to MANIN to take over billets of 6th L.F.

4. All Officers' kits, blankets (rolled in 10's), Coy stores, etc., are to be packed and labelled and d/d *dumped* at Batt. QM. stores by 12 noon.

5. A loading party of 1 NCO. and 2 O/R from each Coy and HQ., under 2/Lt. Turner will report at QM. Stores at time to be notified later. This party will march in rear of the Battn. and be responsible for the unloading on arrival at MANIN.

6. 1st and 2nd Line Transport will move under Transport Officer. Particulars of extra transport available will be issued to Q.M. and T.O. later.

7. Marching out states of Coys. to be sent to Orderly Room by 12 noon, and marching in states to HQ. at MANIN half an hour after arrival.
   Further details will be given at Conference at 11 a.m. today, at which all OC Coys, OC HQ, T.O., and QM. will attend.

8. 9th Gloucester Regt. will be taking over billets here.

                                                      Capt. and
                                                      Adjutant.

Copy No. 1 to OC A Coy.
 "   " 2 " " B "
 "   " 3 " " C "
 "   " 4 " " D "
 "   " 5 " " HQ "
 "   " 6 " T.O.
 "   " 7 " Q.M.
         8   War Diary
         9   War Diary

APPENDIX No 6.

PAMPHLET DROPPED FROM ENEMY PLANES

Appendix No 4.

Brigade Scheme.

War Diary

GENERAL IDEA.

An Eastern force is operating against a Western force. The Western force has been driven out of its trench system and has been fighting a rearguard action for 4 days and is endeavouring to fight a delaying action to give time for completion of its defences further West.

SPECIAL IDEA.

The 66th Division is advancing on ST POL by 2 roads, with 198th Infantry Brigade on ARRAS - ST POL Road and 199th Infantry Brigade on the HABARCQ - IZEL les HAMEAU - PENIN - MAIZIERES Road. South African Brigade in reserve following in rear of the 199th Infantry Brigade.

On night of 25/26th the 66th Division is holding an outpost line from ARRAS - ST POL Road (inclusive) South of AUBIGNY to NOYELLETE inclusive having been employed on 25th instant for the first time.
The 243rd Infantry Brigade is on the left of the 199th Infantry Brigade.

Orders are received from XXV CORPS that pursuit will be continued at dawn on 26th inst.

FOR INSTRUCTIONAL PURPOSES ONLY.   Copy No. 3

9th. BATTN. MANCHESTER REGT.
ORDER No.

Ref: LENS. 1/100,000.   25th. September, 1918.

1. **INFORMATION.**
   (a) The enemy is expected to continue his delaying actions tomorrow and his resistance is likely to stiffen as he approaches ST. POL.
   (b) No fresh divisions have been identified on the 66th Division front during the day, but the 19th Reserve Division which is opposite the Brigade front still has one regiment which has suffered very few casualties.

2. **INTENTION.**
   (a) The advance will be continued tomorrow. The 199th Infantry Brigade will move on the IZEL-LES-HAMEAU - FM. DOFFINE - PENIN - MAIZIERES - MONT-EN-TERNOIS Road as shown on the attached table.
   (b) The 193th Infantry Brigade is moving on ARRAS - ST POL Road. (imaginary).
   (c) The 243rd Infantry Brigade is moving on WANQUENTIN - AVESNES-LE-COMTE - DENIER - MAGNICOURT-SUR-CANCHE Road. (imaginary).
   (d) The South African Bde. is in reserve to 66th Div. and is moving in rear of 199 Infy. Bde. (imaginary)

3. **ADVANCE GUARD.**
   (a) Advance Guard Commander. Major C.F.F. DAVIES, 5th Bn. Connaught Rangers.
   (b) Composition of Advance Guard.
       2 Coys. 5th Connaught Rangers.
       1 Section 'A' M.G. Coy. (imaginary).
       1 Artillery Patrol. (imaginary)

4. **OUTPOST.**
   The outpost of 18th (L.H.Y.) Kings Liverpool Regiment will be withdrawn as soon as the 5th Connaught Rangers have passed the starting point. (imaginary).

5. **CAVALRY.**
   There are no cavalry to be employed on 66th Division front.

6. **TANKS.**
   No tanks are being employed on 66th Division front.

7. **AEROPLANES.**
   Contact Aeroplanes will be flying during the advance and care must be taken to light flares when called by contact aeroplanes to do so.

8. **COMMUNICATION.**
   (a) Visual. Communication will be established by means of visual signalling whenever possible between Battn. H.Q. and Bde. H.Q. and between Battn. H.Q. and Coys.
   (b) Lieut G.E. CURWEN will report, mounted, to Bde. H.Q. as Liaison Officer and will be accompanied by 2 cyclists. He will ride with Bde. H.Q. at the head of the main body.

9. **ANTI-AIRCRAFT PROTECTION.**
   Coys are responsible for their own A.A. defence on the line of march.

10. **STARTING POINT.**
    Where railway crosses road about 200 yds S of L: HAMEAU. Battn. will pass starting point at 6.19 a.m. in following order:-
    H.Q. C, D, B, A Coys, Transport. Sch. A in rear.

11. TRANSPORT.
Echelon A. will move in rear of Battn. under Transport Officer. Echelon B. will not move with the Battn.

12. MEDICAL.
The tent sub-division of 2/3rd E.L. Field Ambulance will establish a hospital at HABARQ. This will be open from 6.0am tomorrow (imaginary).

13. AMMUNITION.
120 rounds S.A.A. will be carried on the man.

14. LOADS.
1st Line Transport will carry its normal loads.

15. SYNCHRONISATION OF WATCHES.
Brigade Signal Officer will synchronise watches at 2.30am on 26th inst.

16. REPORTS.
All reports to Battn. H.Q.

17. Issued by cyclist orderly at 7.0.pm.

L. A. Tunay.

Captain and Adjutant.
9th Bn. Manchester Regt.

DISTRIBUTION:-
Copy No 1. Commanding Officer
2)
3) War Diary.
4 OC A Coy
5 " B "
6 " C "
7 " D "
8 " HQ " and Signal Officer.
9 Medical Officer
10 Transport Officer
11 Q.M.
12 File.

Major R.M.C.Scott MC

O.C. "A" "B" "C" "D" "H.Q". T.D. Q.M.
War Diary.(2). M.O.

War Diary

Herewith Operation Orders for Scheme tomorrow.

1. For the purpose of the exercise all times given in attached orders will be put on three hours.

2. The intention is to practice the following:-

    (a). Attack formations and initiative of commanders.

    (b). Communications.

    (c). Writing of messages.

    (d). Ammunition supply.

3. The enemy will be represented by white flags each flag representing a post of 2 light Machine Guns with its compliment of infantry up to a strength of one platoon.
These flags will be waved when the enemy is actually firing but will otherwise not be shown.

4. Each Battalion will be accompanied by an Umpire who will inform Battalion when they are under Artillery fire.

5. Care must be taken not to damage roots, potatoes or other crops.

6. When the "Cease Fire" is sounded all troops will form up and march home. Half an hour after the "Cease Fire" has sounded Bn. Commanders, 2nd in Command, Adjutants and Coy. Commanders will meet the Brigade Commander at the Mill W. of the GIVENCHY-VILLERS -SIR-SIMON Road.

7. All troops will march in fours on the line of march.

8. Further signal instructions will be issued by the Brigade Signal Officer tonight.

9. G.S.O.1., G.S.O.2. and G.S.O.3 are acting as Umpires.

10. D R E S S.
Battle Order. Steel Helmets. Waterbottles to be filled.

L.A. Turvey

Captain and Adjutant.
9th Battalion MANCHESTER REGIMENT.

25.9.18.

9TH BATTALION,
MANCHESTER REGT.
No. MN 990
Date 25 SEP 1918

Appendix No 8

Operation Order No 3

SECRET.   Operation Order N° 3   Copy N° 3

By Lieut-Colonel. J.J.B. Morrell. M.V.O.
Commanding 9th Battalion. the Manchester Regiment.
                                                                    28. 9. 17.
Reference Map LENS. 11. 1/100,000.

1. The Battalion will move from First Army Area to Fourth Army Area, to-morrow, 29th inst.

2. The Battalion will parade at Starting Point ready to move off to TINCQUES STATION. Head of Column to be at Starting point ready to move off at 8.0. a.m. in the following order. H.Q. D Coy. BAND, B, A, C. Coys. Marching in threes.

3. Starting Point :- Junction of IZEL-LEZ-HAMEAU. Road and Battalion H.Qrs. Road.

4. DRESS. Full marching order, water bottles filled. Helmets and Ground Sheets on packs. Mugs are not to be carried on the outside of packs or haversacks.

5. ROUTINE   Reveille. 5.30 a.m.
              Sick parade. 6.0 a.m.
              Breakfast. 6.15 a.m.
    Blankets at Q.M Stores }   Officers Kits   }
    rolled in bundles of 10 & labelled } 6.45.a.m. at Q.M Stores } 7.0. a.m.

6. RATIONS. The meat and potatoes for to morrow's rations will be cooked to-night, issued to the men & placed in canteens for consumption in the train.
    Remaining Rations - Rice etc - will be carried on the lorries. Rations for Sunday will be issued on arrival at New Billets.

7. COOKS. 1 Cook per Coy and H.Q. will report with Camp Kettles at QM Stores at 7.30 am & will travel with QMs loaders on lorries & have tea ready on arrival of Battalion at Destination. Remainder of Cooks will march with the Battalion.

8. Pioneers, Shoemakers, Tailors and all H.Q employ, less loaders, will march with Battalion.

9. On arrival at TINCQUES STATION. men will be entrained, placing their kits in the trucks. Platoons will then fall in and fill water bottles.
    No man is allowed to leave the Station on any pretext whatever, but must remain at his truck on the train.

10. Marching Out States will be submitted to B.O.R. by 6.0. am.

Issued at 3.30 pm
Distribution. Nos Commdg Officer
              2 Second in command
              3 War Diary.
              } Coys
              } O.C.
              } T.O.
              } Q.M.
              } Signal Officer (O.S. M.O.M.)
              } T.O.

                                            L. A. Turvey.
                                            Captain and Adjutant.
                                            9th Battalion, Manchester Regiment.

Appendix No. 9.

Operation Order No 4.

OPERATION ORDER, NUMBER 4.
by Lt Col J. F. B. MORRELL, MVO.
Commanding 9th Battalion Manchester Regiment.

Reference Map - AMIENS 17, 1/100,000

1. The Battalion will move to PROYART sub-area to-morrow 29th instant
2. Coys. will parade at Starting Point at 8XXX 10.15.am ready to march off in the following order
   H.Q. "D" "B" Band "A" "C" Coys. Transport.
3. Starting Point "C" Coys Billets. Breakfast 7.30.a.m.
4. Rputine - Reveille 6.30.a.m.
   Sick Parade 8.a.m.
   Blankets, Officers Kits, Mess Boxes of all Coys 8.0.a.m. at Battn Orderly Room
5. Haversack rations to be carried. Waterbottles to be filled.
   Road restrictions do not allow of a halt to be made for midday meal.
6. Water cart will be filled by 8.0'a.m. for filling men's water bottles. Water for cooking will be drawn from pumps in billets.
7. An advance party consisting of Lieut. A.H. ALLEN, C.Q.M.S.'s of Coys including H.Q. Coy. will parade at Battn. H.Q. on BICYCLES at 9.0. am in order to meet Staff Captain at PROYART CHURCH at 11.0. a.m.

(Signed) L. A. TURVEY.
Captain and Adjutant.
9th Battn. Manchester Regt.

Issued at. 11. 30 p.m.
28/9/18.

Major Scott

O.C. A, B, C, D, H. QCoys T.O. & Q.M.

Reference Operation Order No.4. para No.2. of 28.9.18.

    The time for moving off will be 10.30.a.m. not 10.15.a.m.

There will be a conference at Headquarters Mess at 10.a.m. of Company Commanders.

                                (sgd) L.A. TURVEY. Capt. and Adjt.,
                                    9th Battalion Manchester Regiment

28.9.18.

Appendix No. 10.

Operation Order No 6

OPERATION ORDER NO. 5.

BY LIEUT. COL. J.F.R. MORRELL. M.V.O.

COMMANDING 9th BATTN. MANCHESTER REGT.

REFERENCE MAP - AMIENS 17 1/100,000

1. The Battalion will move to MARICOURT area to-morrow 1st October 1918

2. Companies will parade at Starting Point at 11.30.a.m. ready to march off in following order - Band, H.Q., B, D, C, A Coys Transport.

3. Starting Point Battalion Headquarters.

4. ROUTINE - REVEILLE 6.a.m. BREAKFAST 7.a.m. SICK PARADE 7.30.a.m. Blankets, Officers Kits, Mess Boxes of all companies to be at Q.M. Stores at 8.30.a.m.

5. Sick will be collected by 8.a.m.

6. Baggage waggons will report to Units by 8.a.m. and will rejoin 544 Coy A.S.C. by 10.30.a.m.

7. Detail of lorries not known.

8. Rations will be delivered to Units on arrival in new area

9. Haversack rations to be carried. Water-bottles filled.

10. Water carts will be filled at 7.30.a.m. for filling men's water bottles. Water for cooking will be drawn from wells in billets.

11. An advance party consisting of Lt ALLEN, CQMSs of companies including H Q, will parade at Battalion Headquarters at 8.30.a.m. in order to meet Staff Captain at Cross Roads 200x west of the "M" of MARICOURT at 11.a.m.

30th Sept 1918

Issued at 11.p.m.

Capt. and Adjt.,
9th Battalion Manchester Regiment

CONFIDENTIAL

WAR DIARY

OF

9½ Bn THE MANCHESTER REGT.

FROM 1st to 31st OCTOBER 1918

VOLUME No 4 — No 10.

Army Form C. 2118.

WAR DIARY / INTELLIGENCE SUMMARY

(Erase heading not required.)

2/6 Manchester Regt.

October 1918

Place	Date	Hour	Summary of Events and Information	Remarks and references to Appendices
PROYART	1-10-18		Battalion marched to MARICOURT and billeted in old tin huts. The 66th DIVISION is now in 4th Army and 13th CORPS. CAPT F.O. THORNE M.C. having joined the Battalion is taken on strength and posted to "C" Coy.	Ref Maps FRANCE AMIENS 1/1 VALENCIENNES 1/2 ST QUENTIN R.
MARICOURT	2-10-18		Headquarters Staff and Coy Commanders reconnoitred training ground in afternoon. Subaltern Officers laid out tape lines by day in the afternoon and Battalion afterwards formed up and carried out an attack. Tea was cooked on the ground. Subaltern Officers again laid out tape lines after dark in some new clearings, and the Battalion formed up by night on these lines. Extract London Gazette No 30876 d: 07-5-18 T/Lieut V.H.P. de SMIDT to be Lieut 1st July 1918, but not to reckon for pay and allowances prior to 13th July 1918.	Appendix 1
-do-	3-10-18		Battalion practised an attack in open warfare assisted by tanks represented by flags. Operation Order No 6 (Appendix No 1) issued at 21.15 hrs.	Appendix 2
-do- MOISLAINS	4-10-18		Battalion marched to MOISLAINS. T/Lieut J. BYRNE is struck off the strength on proceeding to M.G. School GRANTHAM. Winter time will come into use on the night 5/6 October 1918. At 01.00 hrs 1.10 am Summer Time on 6 Oct the clock will be put back one hour. The following is kit order and carried : all Pouches ammunition on the point- Rifle & sling Equipment (with pack- bayonet Haver Tin Water Bottle, 120 rds S.A.A. Steel Helmet S.B.R Rifle & Sling (Chief Ration or Extra day's Ration) Cardigan, 2 Pr Socks, Towel, Soap, Holdall, Oil Tin, Iron Ration, 1 day's Ration Waterproof Sheet. LIEUT J.F. BRISTER is struck off strength of joining 3rd Army Provost Reinforcement Officer. Operation Order No 7 (Appendix No 2) issued at 01.28 hrs. Battalion moved to TEMPLEUX-LA-FOSSE	Appendix 3
-do-	5-10-18		Battalion remaining at MOISLAINS.	

Army Form C. 2118.

WAR DIARY
INTELLIGENCE SUMMARY.

(Erase heading not required.) 9% B Manchester Regt

October 1918.

Place	Date	Hour	Summary of Events and Information	Remarks and references to Appendices
MOISLAINS & TEMPLEUX-LA-FOSSE	5-10-18 (cont)		Battalion was at TEMPLEUX-LA-FOSSE by about 13.00 hrs.	REF. MAPS FRANCE. AMIENS 17 ST. QUENTIN 7. VALENCIENNES 1:100,000
do	6-10-18		Battalion organised and prepared to move.	
do	7-10-18		Battalion moved via LONGAVESNES and RONSOY to HINDENBURG LINE and rested during night in shelters in Canal Tunnel E of BONY. Operation Order no 2 Appendix no 3 issued.	Appendix no 33
			Battalion took part in Operations from 8th to 11th October 1918. Description of these operations given in Appendix no 4.	Appendix no 4.
REUMONT	11-10-18		Battalion relieved in the line by the 2nd Bn NORTHUMBERLAND FUSILIERS before midnight and moved into rest billets at REUMONT.	
"	12-10-18		The Battalion "B" Teams rejoined from MOISLAINS at 10.00 hrs headed by the Battalion Band. During the afternoon REUMONT was shelled with H.E. and BLUE CROSS. 1 O.R. killed & 30 OR wounded	Appendix lost
MAUROIS	13/10/18		Operation Order no 9 issued (Appendix no 5) Battalion moved to MAUROIS. Church Service as usual on arrival. Battalion reorganising. Copy of same from 66th Div. under "G.O.C. and Staff E.d.C. offer congratulations on successful operation." 1 O.R. wounded.	
do	14-10-18		Training and reorganisation. CAPT J DUNCAN in stead of the effective strength on proceeding to BASE and ceasing to be attached to 199th INF BDE HQ.	
do	15-10-18		Training and reorganisation.	

Army Form C. 2118.

WAR DIARY
INTELLIGENCE SUMMARY.
(Erase heading not required.)

2nd Bn Manchester Regt.

October 1918.

Instructions regarding War Diaries and Intelligence Summaries are contained in F. S. Regs., Part II. and the Staff Manual respectively. Title pages will be prepared in manuscript.

Place	Date	Hour	Summary of Events and Information	Remarks and references to Appendices
MAUROIS	16-10-18		Training and reorganisation. From 06:00 hrs tomorrow the Battalion will be under 2 hours notice to move. Owing to the enemy's retirement and to the present fighting it is highly probable that the enemy has left agents behind him, also that he will take every opportunity to send agents and spies among us. We are hence to be very careful in our dealings with civilians & if the Coy should take up billets to see that no documents that might be of value to the enemy are carefully examined.	VALENCIENNES 1:40,000 FRANCE Sht 5/13 1:40,000 [initials]
-do-	17-10-18		Orders received to be ready to move at two hours notice after 05:00 hours.	[initials]
-do-	18-10-18		The Battalion marched out at 02:45 hours to its former position in high ground WEST of LE CATEAU, and remained until 20:50 hours when it moved through LE CATEAU to relieve the 6th Bn LANCS FUS in positions they had occupied the same afternoon in high ground EAST of LE CATEAU in and around K.36. 4 O.R. wounded 1 O.R. missing	[initials]
LE CATEAU K.36.	19-10-18		From the early hours of the morning the battalion position was subjected to M.G. fire and sniping from positions on the S.W. side of RICHEMONT RIV. At 9 a.m. a post of "A" Coy was messing with the exception of one man who was able to run away from the enemy patrol. Later in the day enemy batteries fired on our positions and inflicted a considerable number of casualties. 2/Lieut. R. SMITH was killed & Lt. F.O. THORPE M.M. was wounded. 2 O.R. killed 2 O.R. wounded.	[initials]
-do-	20-10-18		Enemy Artillery fire increased and an attempt by a platoon of "C" Coy and a platoon of "D" Coy to establish a post on the RICHEMONT RIV. was repelled by M.G. fire. Lieut. J. SCHOFIELD was wounded. 8 O.R. and a number of O.R. Casualties 1918 + 20 ft more whom W.O.	

WAR DIARY

INTELLIGENCE SUMMARY.

Army Form C. 2118.

9th Bn. The Manchester Regt.

October 1918.

Place	Date	Hour	Summary of Events and Information	Remarks and references to Appendices
LE CATEAU 11°36' to MAUROIS	20-10-18 (contd)		The Battalion was relieved by the 7th (R.) WEST KENT REGT and moved to the vicinity at MAUROIS. 6 O.R. killed. 2 Lieut J SCHOFIELD and 14 O.R. wounded. 2 O.R. missing, 1 O.R. died of wounds.	FRANCE/Sheet 57/C 1:40,000 VALENCIENNES 1:100,000
ELINCOURT	21-10-18		The Battalion marched to ELINCOURT for a period of rest and reorganised on the basis of 3 platoons per coy. Capt FITZANDOR M.C. having rejoined the Battalion assumed command of "B" Coy vice W. FAIR Bey not having found the effective strength and posted to "B" Coy with 2 Lt PH 1776 Capts the Battalion was then on the effective strength.	
do	22-10-18		Latest from orders. The B.O.C. wishes to express his thanks to all ranks for the work done in the recent fighting. He is very proud of the successful beginning made by the 199 Brigade which showed invaluable for initiative shown by all Commanders, both Officers and NCOs. Taken advantage of by the presence of the men. Enabled us to exploit success and resume quickly future operations.	
do	23-10-18		Companies were inspected by the Commanding Officer. A draft of 149 O.R. rejoined from the Battalion. Capt J GEEN having rejoined the Battalion was to be effective strength and posted to "C" Coy with effect from today.	
do	24-10-18		Companies were inspected by the Commanding Officer after which Lewis Gun training commenced under 2 Lt PH DAVIES at H.Q. "B" Coy are arranged as under - "A" Coy 25 O.R. "B" Coy 10 O.R. "C" Coy 26 O.R. "D" Coy 25 O.R.	
do	25-10-18		Inspection and Route march. Ant. Tank and Gas instruction will be commenced tomorrow.	

Army Form C. 2118.

WAR DIARY
INTELLIGENCE SUMMARY.
(Erase heading not required.)

October 1918. 1st Bn. The Manchester Regt.

Place	Date	Hour	Summary of Events and Information	Remarks and references to Appendices
ELINCOURT	26-10-18		Inspection by G.O.C. Brigade.	Sketch map VALENCIENNES 1:100,000
-do-	27-10-18		Brigade Church Service.	
-do-	28-10-18		Brigade Route March & Transport.	
-do-	29-10-18		Divisional Commanders Inspection cancelled, training instead.	
-do-	30-10-18		Brigade Field Day.	
-do-	31-10-18		Divisional Scheme. Battalion could not attend on acc. distance of frontage &c. and scheme noted in full to take place in the future. The health of the Battalion is very good and the moral of the men excellent. The Effective Strength of the Battalion is 29 Officers and 835 O.R.	

J.P.S Kennedy Lieut Col.
Comdg 1st Bn The Manchester Regt

Appendix No 1.

Operation Order No 6

SECRET   Copy No. 2

OPERATION ORDER, NUMBER 6.
by
LIEUT COLONEL J. P. E. MORRELL MVO.
Commanding, 9th Battalion, Manchester Regiment

3.10.18.

REFERENCE MAP - ~~1/20,000~~ 62C 1/40,000

1. The Battalion will move to-morrow to MOISLAINS. Distance about 9 miles.

2. Starting Point - Cross Roads A.21.b.2.7.

3. Following will be order of march for companies. Head of column to be at starting point at 0700 hours - H.Q. Band, A, D, B, C, Coys, Transport.

4. Billetting party consisting of Lieut R. HALLIDAY, C.QMS of companies and representatives of H.Q. and Transport will proceed to MOISLAINS on bicycles. This party will assemble at Battalion H.Q. at 0730 hours and meet Staff Captain at Area Commandant's Office, MOISLAINS at 0900 hours.

5. (a) Lewis Gun Limbers and Coy. Mules will follow the company to which they belong on line of march.
   (b) Remainder of 1st and 2nd line Transport will move under orders of T.O, 35 yards interval to be kept between each section of six vehicles.
   (c) One lorry is allotted to the Battalion and can be used for two journeys. Q.M. to detail guide to conduct lorry from Brigade H.Q. at 0645 hours to Battalion H.Q.

6. Sick will be collected at 0700 hours to-morrow.

7. Routine - REVEILLE 0500 hours   SICK PARADE 0545 hours.
            BREAKFAST 0600 hours   Blankets (rolled in 10s)
   Officers' Kits, Mess Boxes of all coys. to be at
   Q.M. Stores at 0630 hours

8. Rations for 5th instant will be issued in new area.

9. Water carts to be filled by 0630 hours and left in Transport Lines. All water bottles are to be filled for the march.

10. Companies will march in threes, 100 yards interval to be kept between companies.

11. Marching Out State to be at O.R. by 0600 hours.

12. Marching in State showing number of men (if any) who fell out on the line of march will be sent to Orderly Room immediately on arrival.

L A Turvey
Captain and Adjutant.
9th Battalion Manchester Regiment

Issued at 2115 hours.

Copies to -   1 Commanding Officer.   2, 3, War Diary.
              4 O.C. "A" Coy.   5   O.C. "B" Coy.
              6 O.C. "C" Coy.   7   O.C. "D" Coy.
              8 H.Q. Coy.   9   T.O.
              10 Q.M.   11 M.O.
              12 R.S.M.

Appendix No 2.

Operation Order No 7.

Copy.

Operation Order No 7.
9th Bn Manchester Regt.

4 - 10 - 18.

Ref Map - Sheet 2

(1) The Battn will move tomorrow 5th inst to TEMPLEUX-LA-FOSSE.

(2) Order of march. H.Q., C, A, D, B Coys. Head of column to be at starting point at 10.00 hours.

(3) Starting point. On road at troughs near Battalion H.Q.

(4) Routine :- Reveille 06.00 hrs. Breakfast 07.00 hrs, Sick Parade 07.30 hrs. Officers Kits and blankets rolled in twos to be at Q.M. Stores at 08.00 hrs. Mens spare kits, haversacks and caps to be at Q.M. stores at 08.15 hrs. Badges to be collected by coys in sacks, (excluding Transport) and placed with spare kit.

(5) Dress. - Battle Order, with greatcoats in pack - Waterbottles full.

(6) All band instruments to be dumped at Q.M. stores by 08.30 hrs.

(7) Light Duty men will parade at Bn H.Q. at 09.00 hrs and proceed to destination under 2Lieut W.R.H. DAVIES

(8) Billeting Party as detailed in operation Order No 6. will report at Bn. H.Q at 08.00 hrs under 2Lieut F. HALLIDAY.

(9) (Inter transference of men to make up Coys.)

(10) Marching out states to Orderly Room by 09.00 hrs. Marching in states, showing number of men who fall out (if any) to be rendered to Orderly Room immediately on arrival.

(11) "B" teams of companies will remain in present camp under Major R.M.L. SCOTT M.C., also the following Officers :-
 CAPT F.O. THORNE M.C.   CAPT. J.P. GOLDSCHMIDT
CAPT G.T. NEWMAN (Leave) Lieut J. TREVIVIAN (Course)
2Lieut E.F. LAIRD 2Lieut H. SMITH, 2Lieut. E. LEES 2Lieut C. GROVES (course)
2Lieut P.H.H DAVIES (To return from destination after conducting party).

(Sd) L A TURVEY Capt & Adjt
9th Bn Manchester Regt.

Issued at 0120 hrs 5-10-18

Copies No 1. - C.O.
  " 2/3 - War Diary.
  " 4/8 - All Coys.
  " 9 - T.O.
  " 10 - Q.M.
  " 11 - S.O.
  " 12 - R.S.M

Appendix No 3.

Operation Order No 8.

SECRET   Copy No. 3

9th Bn. Manchester Regt.
Operation Order No. 8.
By Lieut Col J.F.B. Morrell M.V.O.

General Plan. 1. A general attack is taking place on a wide 7-10-18.
front. The XIII Corps Sector as shown on the maps issued with 2nd American Corps on the Right, and 5th Corps (3rd Division) on left.
The date of attack is 8th October 1918.

Corps Plan 2. Forming up line on 13th Corps front is shown in black on maps issued to you today.
(a) The attack to the first objective (RED line) is being made by the 66th Division on a two Brigade front in conjunction with 7th Brigade (25th Division) on the Right and 149th Brigade (50th Division) on the left.
Dividing lines as shown on maps issued.
(b) The capture of the 2nd objective (GREEN line) is being made by 66th Division on a one Brigade front. At the same time the 2nd American Corps is to capture PREMONT

Assembly. 3.(a) The 199th Brigade with 432nd Field Coy. R.E. and 'D' Coy 25th M.G. Battn. will be concentrated by 14.00 on Y day in the HINDENBURG LINE in A.15.d. and A.21.b.
(b) ZERO HOUR. 05.10. - 8-10-18.
(c) At Z - 1½ hours the head of the column will pass cross roads A.16. - 7.7. and will move along the line A.15.d.9.5. - A.17.c.9.4. - A.18.d.0.0. - S of TORRENS CANAL. - MUSHROOM QUARRY (B.20.a.5.8.) - WEST of BELLE VUE FARM to assembly positions in rear of BEAUREVOIR - GUISANCOURT FARM Road in the following order:-
   9th Manch. R. and Attached Units.
   5th Connaught R. and Attached Units.
   18th (LN) Kings Liv. R.
   199th Brigade HQ and Signal Sections
   432nd Field Coy. R.E. (less two sections)
   'D' Coy. 25th M.G. Battn. (less   sections)
   199th L.T.M.B.
(d) Assembly positions are shown on the maps issued.
(e) Coys will report arrival in assembly positions.
(f) Coys will move up in threes each with a guide at distances of 100 yds.

Attack. 4. The attack on the GREEN line, will be carried out. with the 5th Connaught R. on the Right and 9th Manch. R. on the Left.
Leading troops will cross the RED Line at Z + 2¼ hs. i.e. as soon as the barrage lifts. They will not leave their assembly positions before Z + 1 hr.
The attack will be directed by Left of 5th Conn. Rangers.

Movement from Assembly Positions.
5. Attacking Battns. will move in Artillery Formation with advance guards from the assembly position to the RED line with left of the 5th Conn. R. and the right of the 9th Manch. R. keeping in touch in the road BELLE VUE FARM – LA SABLONNIERE – PTE FOLIE FARM. They will keep as close formations as shelling conditions will allow.
All officers will be given a compass bearing to final objective to ensure direction.

Objectives and Boundaries.
6. Battns. are allotted the following objectives and boundaries:-
(a) Objectives.
5th Conn. R. GREEN LINE from U.21.b.7.5. – U.14.b.5.7. including SERAIN.
9th Manch. R.   "   "   "   U.14.b.5.7. – T.12.b.6.1. including high ground N. West of SERAIN.
(b) Boundaries.
5th Conn. R. Right flank. U.25.d.7.4. – U.21.b.7.5.
Dividing line between Battns. U.19.c.8.5. – West side of road from LES FOLIES to SERAIN. – Western outskirts of SERAIN VILLAGE to U.14. Central – U.8.d.6.0.
9th Manch. R. left flank. T.17.a.2.2. – T.12.b.6.1.
Companies.
B Coy. U.14.b.5.7. inclusive to U.7.d.6.4. inclusive.
C "   U.7.d.6.4.   "   " T.12.b.6.1.   "
Support Coy.(A Coy) U.13. Central
Reserve Coy. D Coy U.19.d.0.7.

Consolidation
7. The following important points will be organised as defended localities immediately after capture.
By 5th Conn. R.   U.21.b.0.6.,   U.15.d.0.8.,   Mill (U.14.b.9.8.)
By 9th Manch. R. B Coy. U.8.c.4.3., C Coy. U.7. central
B Coy to get into touch with U.14.b.9.8.
C "   "   "   "   "   6th L.F.s at T.12.b.2.2.

Reserve.
8. The 1/8(L'pl) Kings Liv. R. will be in reserve but until permission is given by the Division they may not be used. They will move in rear of the attacking Battns. by the route detailed in para 6.

Machine Guns.
9. As soon as B & C Coys have captured their objectives on the green line, 2 sections of D Coy, 25th M.G. Battn. will be sent up to B Coy. and 2. V.M.Gs to C Coy. to be used for the defence of the captured objectives.

R.E's
10. As soon as C Coy has captured its objective, 1 section of the 432nd Coy R.E. will be sent to OC C Coy to assist in the consolidation of strong points in U.7. central. When OC C Coy has finished with men, they will be despatched to OC B Coy to assist in the consolidation of strong point U.8.C.4.3.

Aeroplanes
11. Instructions regarding aeroplanes have already been issued to Coys.

Communications
12. Visual Runner and Mounted Orderly Services will be established between Battns. and Bde. HQ.

Headquarters   Headquarters will be established as follows:-
13. (a). Brigade to ZERO :- A.15.d.9.3. with advance report
                centre at MUSHROOM QUARRY.
        ZERO to Z plus 1½ — MUSHROOM QUARRY with advance
        report centre at BELLE VUE.
        ZERO plus 1½ – 2½ · BELLE VUE FARM with advance
        report centre at T.29.a. (cross roads).
        ZERO plus 2½ – 3½. at cross roads T.29.a. with
        advance report centre at PTE FOLIE FARM.

    (b). Battns. will establish their headquarters on the track
        BELLE VUE FARM — LA SABLONNIERE — PTE FOLIE FM. and after
        capture of GREEN line as follows:-
            5th Conn. R.   U.20.a.5.7.
            9th Manch. R. LES FOLIES.

Synchronization   Brigade Signal Officer will synchronise watches at
of Watches   1800 on Y day and at ZERO – 3.
  14.

Acknowledge   Coys will acknowledge immediately on receipt.
  15.

                                L A Turvey
                                Captain and Adjutant.
                                9th Bn. Manchester Regt.

Distribution:-
1. Commanding Officer.
2)
3) War Diary.
4)
5)
6)
7) OC Coys.
8)
9) Signal Officer
9. M.O.
10. T.O.
11. Q.M.
12. OC M.G. Detach.
13. Liaison Officer.
14. R.S.M.
15. File

            The following additional arrangements have been made.
ADDENDUM. 1. Aeroplanes will drop smoke bombs on West exits
            of SERAIN from Z plus 3 hrs. for 20 minutes.
          2. No other smoke is being used on the Brigade
            front.
          3. Contact aeroplanes will call for flares at ZERO plus 2.35,
            ZERO plus 4 hr. and ZERO plus 5 hr.
          4. If only slight resistance is met with on GREEN line being
            taken, 19th and S.A. Bdes. may be required to go through
            again on a two Battn. front, each Bde. about 2000 yds
            frontage. Dividing line U.14 central V.9.d. central.
          5. If enemy is found to have retreated during today,
            19th and S.A. Bdes. may be called upon to take over
            line and follow him up. each on a two Battn. front.

Appendix No 4.

Description of Operations
8th to 11th October 1918.

Description of Operations 8th - 11th October 1918
9th Bn. The Manchester Regt.

Ref maps. Sheet 62 C. 1:40,000 MONTBREHAIN 1:20,000

On October 8th 1918 the Battalion (21 Officers and 708 O.R.) took part in an attack in the XIII Corps sector in conjunction with the V Corps on the left and the 2nd American Corps on the right. As regards the 66th Div: the attack on the first objective was made by the 197th and 198th Inf. Bdes.

The 199th Inf Bde moved from the Hindenburg line and reached assembly positions in rear of the BEAUREVOIR - GUISANCOURT FARM Road at 03.40 hrs. At 06.20 hrs this brigade left the assembly positions and passed through the 197th and 198th Inf Brigades in their objectives at 07.56 hours, at which time the barrage lifted.

The attack by the 199th Inf Bde was carried out with the 5th CONNAUGHT RANGERS on the Right and the 9th Bn MANCHESTER REGT on the Left. The Battalion was allotted objective and boundaries as follows:- Objective (Green Line) from V.14.b.5.7 - T.12.b.6.1 including high ground NW. of SERAIN.

Boundaries:- Right flank:- U.19.c.8.5. W of side of road from LES FOLIES to SERAIN, Western outskirts of SERAIN Village to U.14 central, V.8.d.6.0.

Left flank. T.17.a.2.2. T.12.b.6.1.

The Battalion had few casualties by enemy artillery before passing through the 198th Inf Bde, and encountered M.G. resistance at the PETIT FOLIES farm on the right and LE HAMAGE farm on the left, being reaching the WALINCOURT - AUDIGNY trench which was 198 Bde objective LES FOLIES farm, and reached its objective by about 11.45 hours. 'B' Coy (Rt Coy) was fired upon by enemy field guns at point blank range and also by machine guns firing at our tanks as they came over the skyline. This Company opened fire on the enemy gunners with two Lewis guns, upon which the enemy left his guns and retired.

Owing to the 198th Inf Bde being held up a few hours, the Left flank of the Battalion was in the air from 09.00 hours to 15.00 hrs. The a reserve Coy was used to form a defensive flank until

198th Inf Bde came up on the left.

The following points were organised as defended localities after the objective had been reached :- U.8.c.4.3. and U.7 central.

Prisoners captured by the Battalion during the day numbered 15 and the following guns were also captured, 4.2 Howitzers two, Field guns, 14, Machine guns 6 Anti Tank gun 1.

The casualties were :- Killed Lieut R.J.W. HIBBS and 10 OR, Wounded :- MAJ. J.S. SMYLIE, CAPT F.T. TAYLOR M.C. Lieut HALLIDAY, Lieuts C. TURNER, ~~N~~, FOY, J. SPARKINSON, Lieut HEDGES M.C. and 80 O.R.

Died of wounds :- Lieut J. FAZACKERLEY and 2 O.R.
(24-10-18)

Large numbers of civilians from SERAIN welcomed our men enthusiastically. Supplies of SAA, L.G. magazines, Tools, Wire and Pickets and Drinking water & were brought up by a tank.

From dusk onwards for about three hours enemy aeroplanes dropped bombs on our position at intervals and on the roads and tracks behind.

Dispositions for the night 8th/9th were as follows:-
One Coy ("D") at U 8 C 4.3 with a platoon at U 8 central.
One Coy ("A") at U 7 central with a platoon at LAMPE FARM.
One Coy ("C") support at U 13 Central.
One Coy. ("B" Small) and Bn.H.Q. in reserve in and about LA FOLIE FARM

Patrolling took place hourly on Coy fronts, between Coys, and between units on flanks

October 9th The advance on the Corps front continued and the Battalion was in reserve to the 199th Inf Bde finding mopping up parties of 2 platoons for AVELU and one Coy for MARETZ. The Battalion moved off at 05.20 hrs and advanced rapidly behind the assaulting Battalions and concentrated after the attack on the high ground on the NORTH side of MARETZ. There was some enemy artillery fire and a squadron of enemy planes came over and opened fire with Machine Guns on our positions. Four prisoners were taken by the Battalion in MARETZ.
4 O.R. were wounded.

October 10th. The advance on the Corps front was continued and the Battalion moved off at 02.45 hours along the main road towards LE CATEAU. MAUROIS and REUMONT were passed without incident. The 199th Inf Bde formed up in Artillery Formation, the Batn being in Support to the Brigade.

Enemy artillery was fairly active and fired a number of rounds Blue Cross (Sneezing Gas) causing gas masks to be worn.

The high ground on the S.E. side of LE CATEAU was reached and consolidated.

At 17.30 hours an attack on LE CATEAU village was commenced by the 18th KINGS LIVERPOOL REGT and the 5th CONNAUGHT RANGERS, the latter unit having "C" and "D" Coys of the Battalion attached to them as supports and for mopping up.

The enemy resisted the attack principally with M.Gs, and the attacking troops were withdrawn during the morning of October 11th before dawn, though the platoons of "D" Coy did not return until 10.00 hours.

The Battalion sent two patrols into LE CATEAU and each met large enemy parties in the village, and had to withdraw after "peaceful penetration" from WEST to EAST up to LA SELLE RIVER.

"B" and "D" Coys relieved the CONNAUGHT RANGERS, taking over posts at K 33 c 1.2 and K 33 b.9.a. during the morning. At 20.00 hours the Battalion was relieved by the 2nd Bn NORTHUMBERLAND FUSILIERS and moved with the rest of the Brigade to Rest Billets in REUMONT, the relief being completed before midnight.

Casualties this day, Wounded 2 O.R. Died of Wounds 1 O.R.

On October 7th Lieut K.H. ALLEN and 7 O.R. were wounded whilst in advance taking over for the Battalion, this Officer died of wounds on the 11 October 1918.

The Casualties for the period 7th to 11th Oct, inclusive were as under:—

	Officers	O.R.
Killed	1	10
Wounded	7	98
Died of Wounds	2	3

Owing to excellent staff arrangements the cookers always arrived and the men got two hot meals a day each day.

Appendix No 5

Operation Order No 9

OPERATION ORDER NUMBER 5.
BY LIEUT COLONEL J. F. B. MORRELL. M.V.C.
Commanding 9th Battalion Manchester Regiment

13.10.18.

Reference Map Sheet 57 b.

The Battalion will move to-day to MAUROIS. Starting Point "B" Coy. H.Q.

2. Order of march Band, H.Q., B, C, D, A Coys. Coys. to be on road ready to move off at 1055 hours.

3. T.O. will provide Transport as under :-
   1 G.S. to collect officers kits from all companies H.Q. on main road at 0900 Hours.
   1 G.S. for greatcoats at Headquarters.
   1 Limber for O.R. and Signal stores.
   LIMBERS FOR LG

4. Transport lines will remain in present location.

5. A Party consisting of 2/Lt GROVES and 1 N.C.O. per coy and H.Q. will meet Staff Capt. at MAUROIS Church at 0900 hours. This party will assemble at "B" Coys. H.Q. at 8.15. a.m.

L A Turvey

Capt. and Adjt.,
9th Bn. Manchester Regiment.

Issued to 1. C.O.   2/3 War Diary.   4 - 7 C.C. Coys.
          8 H.Q.   9 T.O.   10. Q.M.   11 R.S.M.

CONFIDENTIAL.

WAR DIARY

OF

9th Bn THE MANCHESTER REGT.

From 1st to 30th November 1918

Volume No 4 —— No 11.

WAR DIARY

INTELLIGENCE SUMMARY

Army Form C. 2118.

(Erase heading not required.)

November 1918. G.H.Q. 2nd Bn. The Manchester Regt.

Place	Date	Hour	Summary of Events and Information	Remarks and references to Appendices
ELINCOURT	1-11-18		Training and Lewis Gun Instruction. Operation Order No 14 issued, the Battalion will move to MAUROIS tomorrow. (Appendix No 1.)	Appendix No 1
do – to MAUROIS	2-11-18		Battalion moved to billets in MAUROIS.	
LE CATEAU	3-11-18		Operation Order No 15 issued. Omitted from own (leaving) The Battalion moved to LE CATEAU. Church Service before leaving.	Appendix No 2
– do –	4-11-18		Battalion rested and packed up, all arrangements to battle order, and prepared for battle. (Zero day Nov 4th 1918) Order No 16 issued (Appendix No 3.)	Appendix No 3
– do –	5-11-18		Battalion marched off at 04.15 hours towards POMEROY. 'B' team and reinforcements remaining at LE CATEAU as attached (Appendix No 4) Battalion reached LANDRECIES.	Appendix No 4
LANDRECIES	6-11-18		Battalion message map of LE CATEAU operation. Battalion moved in the afternoon to MARDILLES and billeted there.	
MARDILLES	7-11-18		Battalion moved to MARBAIX and billeted there.	
MARBAIX	8-11-18		The Battalion moved in Brigade Reserve for GRAND FICHEAU and from there proceeded to LA TUILLERIE, remaining there for the night. In the afternoon 2/Lieut P.A.H. DAVIES and 1 O.R. were wounded whilst moving up as on liaison with 6th CONNAUGHT RANGERS.	
LA TUILLERIE	9-11-18		Battalion left for BAS LIEU of AVESNES. 2/Lieut P.A.H. DAVIES died of wounds.	Appendix No 5
BAS LIEU	10-11-18		Battalion moved to SARS POTERIES. Description of operation 4th – 11th is attached (Appendix No 5)	
SURY	11-11-18		Battalion left line as described in Appendix No 5 with H.Q. in the village. Hostilities ceased at 11.00 hours. Message to all ranks of wishing from General RAWLINSON received (Appendix No 6A)	Appendix No 6A

Army Form C. 2118.

WAR DIARY
INTELLIGENCE SUMMARY.

(Erase heading not required.)

November 1918.   9/B Br. The Manchester Regt.

Instructions regarding War Diaries and Intelligence Summaries are contained in F.S. Regs., Part II. and the Staff Manual respectively. Title pages will be prepared in manuscript.

Place	Date	Hour	Summary of Events and Information	Remarks and references to Appendices
SIVRY.	12-11-18.		Battalion holding the line lightly - a few enemy seen near SIVRY STATION, but nothing occurred. "B" teams arrived from TAISNIERES. A, B, & C Coys will work on main road through SIVRY from "A" Coys Advance Post on SIVRY STATION ROAD to cross roads A.24. b.4.3. Lieut R.R. GRIST and 2/Lt N.J. MARGETTS and 2/Lt E. AITKEN-DAVIES (Devon Regt.) having joined the Battalion are taken on the effective strength and posted to "B", "C" and "B" Coys respectively.	Ref. maps NAMUR 1/100,000.
-do-	13-11-18.		Work on roads and clearing up. No signs of any enemy. Civilians are not allowed to pass through the lines either way. "A" Coy is building an emplacement on the SIVRY STATION ROAD to take the German gun captured by "C" Coy. The emplacement marks the most EASTERLY spot reached by the Battalion on the cessation of hostilities.	
-do-	14-11-18.		A general of Honours consisting of 3 Officers, 4 Sergts and 42 O.R. proceeded to SOLRE LE CHATEAU on the occasion of the visit to that place of the Corps Commander XIII Corps. Military Medals were presented to the under-mentioned :- 5663 Sergt HILL T. "C" Coy, 15727 Cpl TOMLINSS. F. "D" Coy, 62242 Pte HALE A. "C" Coy, 30356 Cpl WINTERBOTTOM. I. "B" Coy, 65005, Pte GASKELL W. "B" Coy, 77776 Pte BEALEY. J. "D" Coy, 17358 Pte GOUGH. H. "B" Coy.	
-do-	15-11-18.		Situation as for 13th preparations commencing for the march to the RHINE. The Division ceased to belong to the XIII Corps with effect from yesterday and now belongs to the IX Corps for the march.	
-do-	16-11-18.		"C" Coy relieved the 5th CONNAUGHT RANGERS in the line, the latter moved to TRIEU-ROUCAUX and 149th Bde H.Q. to CHATEAU at cross roads about 1 mile NORTH of WEST of that place. The SOUTH AFRICAN BRIGADE moved into SIVRY. Instructions for march to RHINE received (Appendix) also Operation Order No 237 and No 24.	Appendix 46.

Army Form C. 2118.

WAR DIARY
INTELLIGENCE SUMMARY.
(Erase heading not required.)

of 1/9th Bn The Manchester Regt

November 1918.

Place	Date	Hour	Summary of Events and Information	Remarks and references to Appendices
SIVRY	17-11-18		Special Order by Lieut. Gen. SIR. T.L.N. MORLAND, K.C.B, K.C.M.G, D.S.O, Cmdg XIII Corps "66th Div. on their leaving XIII Corps:- I wish to express to the G.O.C. and all ranks of the 66th Divn my Appreciation of their gallant and distinguished service during the recent operations which have resulted in complete victory. To each individual of the British, Irish and South African troops composing the Division I express my hearty thanks for his splendid efforts." 2nd Lieut W.N. STODDARD and Lieut C.H. BRABHAM (Devon Regt) having joined the Battalion are posted to "B" "D" and "C" Coys with effect from 16-11-18 and 17-11-18 respectively. 2nd Lieut P. DARLINGTON M.C. having been trans-posted to 20th Batn Manchester Regt. is struck off the effective strength of the Battalion with effect from 16-11-18. The Battalion will move tomorrow to CERFONTAINE. Operation Order No 25 (Appendix No 7) issued.	Ref: Map NAMUR 1:100,000 Appendix 7.
-do- CERFONTAINE.	18-11-18		The Battalion marched to CERFONTAINE and was in Billets at that place at 12 noon.	
-do-	19-11-18		Physical training for Coys and practice of loading waggons and limbers. Special emergency Scheme for preparing the troops to return to civil life commences tomorrow.	
-do-	20-11-18		Work as for 19th. Special Order by Maj. Gen. H.K. BETHELL. C.M.G. D.S.O. Cmdg 66th Div. received (Appendix No 8) Bayonet training, handling arms and work on road to SENZEILLE.	Appendix 8.
-do-	21-11-18		Training and work as for yesterday.	
-do-	22-11-18		Training and work as before. Battalion will probably move to MORVILLE on the 24th inst. Operation Order No 24 (Appendix No 9) issued.	Appendix 9.
-do-	23-11-18		Battalion Parade. Photos frozen to work on. Copy of Special Order of the Day by MARSAL FOCH. "Officers N.C.Os and soldiers of the Allied Armies, After bringing the enemy's attack to a stand by your stubborn defence, you attacked him without respite with unrelenting energy and unwavering faith (Faith)	

WAR DIARY

INTELLIGENCE SUMMARY

9th Bn The Manchester Regt.

November 1918

Army Form C. 2118.

Place	Date	Hour	Summary of Events and Information	Remarks and references to Appendices
CERFONTAINE	23-11-18 (contd)		(contd) "You have won the greatest battle in history and have saved the most sacred of all causes, the Liberty of the World. You may well be proud. You have covered your standards with immortal glory, and the gratitude of posterity will ever be yours." From General MILNE, SALONICA. 12-11-18 "The British Army in the Balkans and to their Comrades in France cordial congratulations and hearty greeting on this great occasion. Reply: "All best thanks to you and the Army under your Command from all ranks of the British Army in France for your welcome message".	Staff Maps NAMUR 1:100,000
- do -	24-11-18		The Battalion marched to MORVILLE (15½ miles) and were billeted in huts and were billets by an enemy aerodrome by 15.00 hours. The village is very small and poor.	
MORVILLE	25-11-18		The Battalion rested and cleaned up.	
- do -	26-11-18		Usual close order and arms drill, and work on roads. Educational Classes for backward men. Battle for the men will be available tomorrow. Picking of cross planes into hanger.	
- do -	27-11-18		Training as for yesterday, also educational classes.	
- do -	28-11-18		Training as for 26th.	
- do -	29-11-18		Battalion parade, ceremonial.	
- do -	30-11-18		Inspection of billets by Commanding Officer, followed by Physical training, Handling of arms and saluting. The weather for the last week has been cold and damp, but in spite of this the health of the Battalion has been very good. The Effective Strength of the Battalion is 31 Officers and 843 O.R.	

MORVILLE
1-12-18

J.H.B. Norvell Lieut Col.
Comdg 9th Bn The Manchester Regt.

Appendix No 1.

Operation Order No 14

SECRET   OPERATION ORDER No. 14   Copy No...
                BY LIEUT COLONEL J. F. R. MORRELL M.V.O.
              COMMANDING 9th BATTALION MANCHESTER REGIMENT

Reference Map — SHEET 57b, 1/40,000

1. The Battalion will move to-morrow, 2nd instant, to MAUROIS.

2. Starting Point — "A" Coy's Headquarters.

3. The head of Battalion will pass Starting Point at 0855 hrs with companies in following order :—
     H.Q., Band, A, B, C, D, Companies.

4. Route. CLARY — BERTRY.

5. Signal Officer will synchronise watches at 0815 hours.

6. Distances on March as in Fourth Army Standing Orders Para 162, to be maintained.

7. Dress — Battle Order with Haversacks. Jerkins to be carried in packs.

8. Blankets and greatcoats, rolled in tens, to be delivered at Q.M. Stores by 0645 hours, and Officers' Kits by 0830 hrs for conveyance by G.S. wagon and lorry allotted the Battn.

9. Orders for Transport will be notified later.

10. Marching Out States to be forwarded to B.O.R. by 0800 hrs. Marching In States to be sent to H.Q. at MAUROIS immediately on arrival.

                                         Capt. and Adjt.,
                                  9th Battalion Manchester Regt.

Copies to:
1. Commanding Officer   2/3 War Diary.
4. O.C. "A" Coy.   5. O.C. "B" Coy.
6. O.C. "C" Coy.   7. O.C. "D" Coy.
8. Headquarters   9. T.O.
10. Q.M.   11. R.S.M.
12. M.O.   13. File.

Appendix No 2.

Operation Order No 15

SECRET　　　　　　　　　　　　　　　　　　　　　　　　　Copy No........

OPERATION ORDER No. 15.
BY LIEUT. COL. J.F.B. MORRELL M.V.O.
COMMANDING 9th BATTN. MANCHESTER REGT.

3/11/18.

Reference Map 57B 1/40,000.

1. The Battalion will move to-day, 3rd inst, to LE CATEAU.

2. Starting Point. "B" Coy. Billet.

3. Route.- REUMONT - PONT DES VEUX (K.33.a') - LE CATEAU.

4. Head of column to be at Starting Point at 1545 hours.
   Coys in following order:-
   H.Q., Band, "B", "A", "D", "C". Coys.

5. Coys at hourly halts will immediately clear the road.

6. Transport.- All Battalion Transport except Coy Limbers, Chargers and Coy Pack animals will be Brigaded under Brigade T.O. and will move under his orders.
   Time for Head of Column to pass Starting Point.- 1710 hours.
   Transport will move straight through without halt.
   Two G.S. Wagons are allotted the Battalion and can be used for more than one journey.

7. Sick are being collected by 2/2 East Lancs. Field Amb.

8. All greatcoats, blankets, and Officers kits to be delivered at Q.M. Stores by 1000 hours. Greatcoats and blankets to be rolled in tens.

9. Normal intervals (Fourth Army Standing Orders, Para 162) will be maintained on line of march.

10. Synchronisation of Watches will be carried out by Battn. S.O. at 1215 hours.

11. Marching Out States to be sent to B.O.R. by 1400 hours.
    Marching In States immediately on arrival in new billets.

　　　　　　　　　　　　　　　　　　　　　　　[signature]
　　　　　　　　　　　　　　　　　　　　　　　Captain and Adjutant.
　　　　　　　　　　　　　　　　　　　　　　　9th Battn. Manchester Regt.

Distribution:-

1. Commanding Officer.　　　11. H.Q. Coy.
2.　　　　　　　　　　　　　　12. R.S.M.
3. War Diary.　　　　　　　　13. File.
4. O.C. "A" Coy.
5. O.C. "B" Coy.
6. O.C. "C" Coy.
7. O.C. "D" Coy.
8. T.O.
9. Q.M.
10. M.O.

Appendix no 3.

Operation Order no 16

SECRET   Copy No......

OPERATION ORDER NO. 38.
BY LIEUT. COL. J.F.B. MORRELL, D.S.O.
COMMANDING 9th BATTN. MANCHESTER REGT.

Ref.Map.   4/11/18.
Sheet 57A.
1/40,000

1. GENERAL ATTACK.
At a date and hour to be notified later operations on a large scale are being carried out.

2. CORPS PLAN
The XIII Corps in conjunction with Corps on either flank is to attack as follows:-
(a) In first phase (up to GREEN LINE)
25th Division on the Right.
50th Division in the Centre.
18th Division on the Left.
66th Division in Corps Reserve.
During this phase the 25th Division is to force the crossing of the canal and operate on the Southern bank, the 50th and 18th Divisions operating North of the canal.
(b) In second phase (up to FINAL OBJECTIVE, BROWN LINE)
66th Division on the Right.
50th Division in the Centre.
18th Division on the Left.
25th Division in Corps Reserve.
During this phase the 66th Division is to pass through the 25th Division. The 50th Div. are to cross the canal and operate on Southern bank, the 18th Div. continuing to operate on the Northern bank.

3. DIVL. PLAN OF ATTACK.
(a) The 66th Div. is to carry out the attack with the 199 Bde on the Right, the 198th Bde. on the Left and the South African Bde. in Divl. Reserve.
(a) The attack up to the BLUE LINE (Road I.15.c.0.0.-&-I.3.c.8.0.) will be carried out by 9th Manchester Regt. In addition at least one bridgehead will be established over the GRAND HELPE RAU, between I.8.b.1.3. and I.3.a.7.2.

4. BRIGADE PLAN OF ATTACK.
The attack will be carried out as follows:-
i. "A" Coy. will secure high ground H.16.b. and if held up will send one Platoon to the South and one Platoon to the North leaving two Platoons on the West to watch while Platoon on the South works round the enemy. "B" and "C" Coys. will move in close echelon to "A" Coy.
ii. "D" Coy will exploit up to high ground on I.14.d.0.0. moving South of the MAROILLES- MARBAIX Road.
iii. "C" Coy to move North of "A" Coy. with its Centre on VALLEZ FARM and from there to Cross Roads in I.7.d. This Coy will capture Southern portion of TASNIERES Village and establish three bridgeheads across the GRAND HELPE RAU with three Platoons South of TASNIERES Rd. and one Platoon North of it. If "C" Coy find strong opposition at the village C.C. "C" Coy will immediately send back to "D" Coy for assistance.
iv. "D" Coy in Battn. Reserve, which will be used to assist "C" Coy if necessary.
(b) The 18th (L.N.Y.) Kings Ldv. Regt.and 5th Connaught Rangers will pass through the 9th Manchester Regt. on the BLUE LINE. The O.C. 18th (L.N.Y.) Kings L'pool Regt. and 5th Connaught Rangers will keep in close touch with O.C. 9th Manchester Regt. and as soon as they are satisfied that the 9th Manchester Regt. are approaching their objective, will pass through without waiting for orders from Brigade H.Q..
(c) As soon as 18th (L.N.Y.) Kings L'pool Regt. and 5th Connaught Rangers have crossed the BLUE LINE the 9th Manchester Regt. will reform and follow 1500 yards in rear of 18th (L.N.Y.) Kings L'pool Regt. as far as I.16.c. where they will remain in Brigade Reserve and get in touch with 97th Bde. 32nd Div. on high ground I.21.central.

Sheet 2.

5. BOUNDARIES (As per maps issued)

Right of Brigade Boundary.- H.17.d.5.7. - I.13.c.0.8. - I.15.c.0.0. - I.25.a.0.4. - I.24.b.4.4. - I.19.a.0.0. - I.19.a.2.2.

Left of Brigade Boundary.- Grid line from H.4.d.4.0. - I.2.c.0.0.

Dividing Line between 18th K.L.R. and 5th Conn. Rngrs. I.9.c.7.0. - I.10.d.9.9. (Bridge inclusive to the Left) thence following GRAND-HELPE EAU to J.13.a.7.0.

Dividing Line between "B" and "C" Coys.- I.9.c.7.7.

6. TACTICAL FEATURES TO BE CAPTURED

Owing to the width of frontage allotted to Battn. it will not be possible to cover the whole ground. Battns. will therefore make for and hold important tactical points such as:
(a) High ground H.18.b.
(b) High ground I.14.d.
(c) River crossings I.3.c. and d., I.9.b.
(d) TASNIERES Village.
(e) DOMPIERRE Village
(f) MARBAIX Village.

7. HEADQUARTERS

Brigade H.Q. will be established at the following places:-
LANDRECIES.
LE PRESEAU.
FERME LE CATILLON.
H.16.b.central.
VALLEY FARM.
I.9.b.0.9.
CHATEAU, I.11.b.

Battalion H.Q. will move in bounds to the following places:
LANDRECIES.
LE PRESEAU.
FERME LE CATILLON.
H.16.b.central.
VALLEY FARM.
CROSS ROADS, I.7.d.
I.15.b. and d.

8. ARTILLERY.

(a) Five Brigades R.F.A. and one Brigade R.G.A. are supporting the attack of the 66th Division.
(b) - Battery of 18Pdrs., and one Section of 4.5. Hows (- Bde R.F.A.) are allotted to 199th Inf. Bde. They will be used as follows:
One Section of 18 Pdrs. is allotted to each Battn. and up to BLUE LINE one Section 4.5. Hows is allotted to 9th Manchester Regt. After capture of BLUE LINE guns and Hows. (One Section 18 Pdrs. and one Section 4.5. Hows) previously allotted to 9th Manchester Regt. will come into Bde. Res.

9. MACHINE GUNS.

One Section of Vickers M.G.s is attached to "B" Coy. and on the capture of high ground in I.14.d. will place two guns in position to assist in the capture of GRAND-HELPE EAU and crossing of same. Two guns will be in reserve to defend against counter attack.

10. R.E.

One Section of 432 Field Coy. R.E. is attached to "C" Coy for throwing over bridges for infantry at the mill in I.9.b.0.9. and North of it. One Section 432 Field Coy R.E. is attached to "D" Coy for construction of bridges for 1st Line Transport.

11. COMMUNICATION

As soon as "A" Coy seize high ground in H.18.b., Sig. Off. will arrange to establish an advance report centre on this high ground. Remainder of Signals remaining with H.Q. This Advance Report Centre will remain in position as a transmitting station until withdrawn. It will get into touch with "B" and "C" Coys and keep touch with same.

Sheet 3.

12. LIAISON ARRANGEMENTS.
(a) The Battn. Liaison Officer will report to Bde. H.Q.
 i. When any of the tactical features mentioned in Para 6 are captured.
 ii. In the event of any unforeseen situation.
In addition Battn. Liaison Officer will report to Bde H.Q. when Battn. crosses GREEN LINE.
"A" and "B" Coys are responsible for keeping liaison with one another and "C" and "D" Coys are responsible for keeping liaison with one another. "C" Coy will also keep touch with 5th Inniskillings Fus. at Chlle DES HAIES (H.12.b.) and in the village of TASNIERES and the crossing of the GRAND-HELPE RAU which is the road from I.15.c.0.0. to I.3.c.8.0.
"D" Coy will also get touch with 108th Bde. at Chlle DES HAIES
"B" Coy to get touch with Cavalry (20th Hussars or 97th Inf. Bde.) on the Right who are exploiting to the line I.14.d.9.0. South along the road to GRANDE FAYT I.28.c., and beyond.
Captain CHADFORD, 6th Dub. Fus., attached to this Bde. will also keep touch with 97th Inf. Bde. on the Right.

13. AMMUNITION PACK MULES.
Coy. pack mules will each carry one box bundle packed S.A.A. for L.G.s and one box ojarger packed S.A.A. for rifles.
T.O. will detail one mule to report to L.T.M.B. to carry T.M. ammunition.

L A Tuvey
Captain and Adjutant.
9th Battn. Manchester Regt.

Distribution:
1. C.O.
2. War Diary.
3.
4. O.C. "A" Coy.
5. O.C. "B" Coy.
6. O.C. "C" Coy.
7. O.C. "D" Coy.
8. O.C. H.Q.
9. S.O.
10. Intell Off.
11. T.O.
12. Q.M.
13. M.O.
14. K.L.R.
15. C.R.
16. File.

Issued by Runner at 1630 hours.

Appendix No 4

Message map of LE CATEAU

MESSAGE MAP

TO :—

I AM AT _____

I AM AT _____ AND AM CONSOLIDATING

_____ AND AM PUSHING FORWARD

I AM TEMPORARY HELD UP AT _____ BY

RIFLE ; M.G FIRE FROM _____

I WANT MORE S.A.A. _____

MY CASUALTIES ARE _____

MY STRENGTH IS _____

INFORMATION ABOUT MY OWN FRONT IS AS FOLLOWS :—
(MARK SITUATION IN ON MAP)

SITUATION ON MY FLANKS APPEARS TO BE :—

I INTEND TO _____

TIME _____

DATE _____

SIGNED _____

REGIMENT _____

500   1000   1000 YARDS

N CORPS TOPO SEC.   MAP Nº 7A.   SCALE 1 : 20,000

Appendix no 5

Description Operations 10th & 11th Nov 1918

REF MAPS.
FRANCE Sheet 57A.
BELGIUM & part of FRANCE : 57 Edn 2
1:40,000

10th Nov. 1918. The Battalion left BAS LIEU for SARS POTERIES at 08.00 hours and went into billets in the latter place. After the mid-day meal, orders were received at 13.00 hours to move to SOIRE LE CHATEAU, and the Battalion moved accordingly. From there it went forward toward RENLIES, starting off at about 15.00 hours. "C" Coy went by CLAIRFAYTS, and from there along the road running N.E. to MOULARD. "B" Coy went via BEAURIEUX along road running E. to MOULARD.

Batn H.Q., "A" & "D" Coys moved by CLAIRFAYTS to CHANT des OISEAUX remaining there for the night.

"B" & "C" Coys met resistance along road on W side of MOULARD running N & S in A.18.d and A.24.b. along the BELGIAN frontier where they were held up.

At 16.35 hours a message was received stating that from a R.A.F. report, the road from EPPE SAUVAGE due S. of SIVRY to TRIEU BOUCHAUX, N.E. of SAUVAGE, was full of enemy transport and guns, and had been bombed and fired on by our planes.

Orders were given for "B" & "C" Coys to endeavour to overcome enemy resistance at W side of SIVRY, and if possible to secure EASTERN and SOUTH EASTERN exits in order that "A" Coy might be pushed through to TRIEU BOUCHAUX, to cut off enemy transport.

As "B" & "C" Coys did not penetrate enemy machine Gun screen until about 03.30 hours Nov 11th, the operation was cancelled.

"B" & "C" Coys spent the night endeavouring to round up enemy Machine Guns. There were no casualties during these operations.

At 03.00 hours on the 11th a patrol of "C" Coy threw a bomb at the enemy Machine Gun at the cross roads A.24.b.4.2. and wounded one of the enemy — the enemy then left their gun.

Before dawn the enemy machine guns on the whole Battalion front became silent, and patrols soon discovered that they were gone.

The advance was continued at 07.00 hours with the 18th Kings (Liverpool) Regt on our right.

The Battalion was ordered to proceed through SIVRY to SIVRY STATION, with right flank guard via VIEUX SART and SAUTAIN, thence to RENLIES. "A" Coy formed the Advanced guard and "D" Coy the right flank guard. "B" & "C" Coys remained in their positions at the western end of MOULARD until SIVRY had been made good by advance guard.

The Battalion moved forward as ordered and the Coys moved along their routes without opposition until they were well beyond SIVRY. "A" Coy was held up on reaching the crest at B.16.d central where fire was opened on it by machine guns and artillery which were not definitely located. "D" Coy reached VIEUX SART without opposition.

In the meantime Bn H.Q. moved to A 24 C. 2.6. and at 10.10 hours, received an order that hostilities would cease at 11.00 hours, this order only reached Coys a few minutes before that hour. Enemy artillery remained active to the last and No 54854 Pte T. FROST of "A" Coy was fatally wounded by a shell less than ten minutes before the armistice commenced.

Disposition of Battalion at commencement of armistice:- "D" Coy Right Coy - one platoon at road junction B.27 d. 3.5. with posts at B 27 d 4.3 and B 27 d 0.0. remainder of Coy in billets near B 27 b. 0.0. "A" Coy (Left) - one platoon at cross roads B 16 d 3.5. with post on road B.16.d. 6.5, B 16 d. 6.7. and B 16 d 4.5. - one platoon at B 15 a. 5.8. with posts at B 15 d. 6.9. and B 15 d. 4.8. remainder of Coy in billets about B 15 d. 0.3. "B" & "C" Coys with Bn H.Q. in billets in SIVRY.

All precautions were taken for defence and strict orders were given regarding fraternisation. At the time of the armistice the Battalion was further EAST than any troops in the 4th Army.

NOTICE

This Gun was captured by "C" Company 1/8th Bart "A" Lesser Regt
at dawn on 11th November 1918
on the spot on which it now stands, attacked by 'C' Company
9/8th Bart Manchester Regt 199th Infantry Brigade, 66th Division
IX Corps British 4th Army at 10 a.m. 11th November 1918

No............ **ACQUITTANCE ROLL (ALL ARMS).** Army Form N. 1513.

{Squadron / Battery / Company} of the ....

Imprest a/c No. ....

ORIGINAL

Regl. No.	RANK AND NAME.	*Adapt if necessary.	Cash Payment		Sterling Equivalent (To be completed in Fixed-Centre Pay Office).		Receipt of Soldier.
			*Francs	Centimes	s.	d.	
		Total					

The undermentioned (¹) and (²) to be completed by Paymaster i/c Clearing House—
s. d.

To be inserted by Paying Officer. Total, in words—

(¹) Rate of Exchange—5 =
(²) Total Sterling equivalent, in words—

Francs .... Pounds.

Centimes .... Shgs., and .... Pence.

Signature of the Officer making the Payments ....

Date of Payment .... 19...... Officer Commanding .... Company.

.... Regiment.

Certified that the above amounts have been charged in the ledger accounts of the men concerned.

Date .... 19...... .... Paymaster.

(21076) Wt. W1593—P1026. 200000 Pads. 5/18. Sir J. C. & S. E. 3165.

Appendix No. 5A.

Gen Rawlinson's message to 4th Army

Fourth Army, No. G.S. 125.

TO ALL RANKS OF THE FOURTH ARMY.

The Fourth Army has been ordered to form part of the Army of Occupation on the RHINE in accordance with the terms of the Armistice. The march to the RHINE will shortly commence, and, although carried out with the usual military precautions, will be undertaken generally as a peace march.

The British Army through over four years of almost continuous and bitter fighting has proved that it has lost none of that fighting spirit and dogged determination which has characterized British Armies in the past, and has won a place in history of which every soldier of the British Empire has just reason to be proud. It has maintained the highest standard of discipline both in advance and retreat. It has proved that British discipline, based on mutual confidence between officers and men, can stand the hard test of war far better than Prussian discipline based on fear of punishment.

This is not all. The British Army has, during the last four years on foreign soil, by its behaviour in billets, by its courtesy to women, by its ever ready help to the old and weak, and by its kindness to children, earned a reputation in France that no army serving in a foreign land torn by the horrors of war, has ever gained before.

Till you reach the frontier of Germany you will be marching through a country that has suffered grievously from the depredations and exactions of a brutal enemy. Do all that lies in your power by courtesy and consideration to mitigate the hardships of these poor people who will welcome you as deliverers and as friends. I would further ask you when you cross the German frontier to show the world that British soldiers, unlike those of Germany, do not wage war against women and children and against the old and weak.

The Allied Governments have guaranteed that private property will be respected by the Army of Occupation, and I rely on you to see that this engagement is carried out in the spirit as well as in the letter.

In conclusion I ask you one and all, men from all parts of the British Empire, to ensure that the fair name of the British Army, enhanced by your exertions in long years of trial and hardship, shall be fully maintained during the less exacting months that lie before you.

I ask you to show the world that, as in war, so in peace, British discipline is the highest form of discipline, based on loyalty to our King, respect for authority, care for the well-being of subordinates, courtesy and consideration for non-combatants, and a true soldierly bearing in carrying out whatever duty we may be called upon to perform.

Rawlinson.
Genl.

H.Q., FOURTH ARMY,
11th November, 1918.   *Commanding Fourth Army.*

Appendix No 6

Instructions for March to RHINE also Operation Orders no 23 & 24.

16-11-18
Copy No. 2

INSTRUCTIONS FOR MARCH TO MAUBE.

1. Composition of Billeting Parties.
Brigade Billeting Party will be composed as follows:-

    1 Officer to be detailed by D.A.Q.
    1 N.C.O. per Coy.
    1 N.C.O. R.E.
    1 N.C.O. Transport.

2. Behaviour on the Line of March.

a. All troops will march in threes.
b. Distances as laid down in F.S. Pocket Book (page 44) will be maintained.
c. Smoking will only be allowed at halts.
d. 1 orderman will follow in rear of each limber.
e. Watermen will follow water carts, and cooks will follow field kitchens. Cooks and Ordermen may put their packs on the field kitchens and limbers but all other men will march fully equipped with the exception of the Band.
f. Men marching with Transport will keep in the Column and will not hang on to vehicles.
g. Mess tins and bags will be carried in the pack.
h. Box Respirators will be carried resting on the pack.
i. Exact method of carrying the blanket and leather jerkin will be notified later.

3. Transport.

a. Coy pack animals and Coy limbers will march in rear of Coys.
b. 1st Line Transport will follow in rear of Battalion in following order:-
                    S.A.A. Limbers.
                    Tools.
                    Maltese Cart.
                    Officers Mess Cart.
                    Water Carts.
                    Cookers.
                    Unauthorised Vehicles.
                    Spare Animals.
c. 2nd Line Transport (including the 4 additional G.S. Wagons which are being sent to Battalions) will follow in rear of 1st Line Transport.
d. Care will be taken that wagons are not overloaded as roads are hilly and reported to be in bad condition.
   The additional G.S. Wagon per Battalion will carry Greatcoats, one days extra rations, reserve of 100x pairs boots, and 1 sackof blanket per man.
e. Particular attention will be paid to Frosts Cogs fitting stage.
f. Coys proceeding in advance of Main Body will take cookers and Water cart.

4. Medical.

a. 1/3rd E.L. Field Ambulance will detail two ambulances to follow in rear of the column.
b. Men will be collected two hours before the head of Main Body passes Starting Point.

5. Synchronisation of Watches.

Brigade Signal Officer will arrange to synchronise watches at 0800 and 2000 hours daily.

6. **Accommodation.**

   It is understood that during part of the march accommodation will be scarce. Arrangements are being made to carry forward on lorries 100 trench shelters per Battalion.

7. **Messes.**

   From the time of move onwards Battalions will arrange to have Battalion Messes instead of Coy Messes whenever possible.

8. **Leave.**

   Leave will continue as usual. Officers and O.R. proceeding on leave will return on empty supply lorries. Returning leave parties will be sent up by supply lorries.

9. **D.A.D.O.S.**

   D.A.D.O.S. will not be able to provide stores throughout the period of the move.

10. **Reporting Arrival.**

    Coys will pay special attention to reporting arrival immediately on arrival at new destination.

    L.A. Twomey

    Captain and Adjutant.
    5th Battn. Manchester Regt.

Distribution:- Normal.

OPERATION ORDER NO. 25.
BY LIEUT. COL. J.P.E. BORRELL V.V.C.
COMMANDING 9th BATTN. MANCHESTER REGT.   16/4.1/19

The Battn., less "C" Coy will remain in present location.

"C" Coy will take over by 1000 hours to-day, posts held by
5th Connaught Rangers.
Strictest March Discipline is to be maintained.
DRESS BATTLE ORDER. HELMET will be worn in lieu of cap.
Completion of relief will be reported to H.Q.

L A Finny

Captain and Adjutant.
9th Battn. Manchester Regt.

SECRET.   Copy No. 2......

OPERATION ORDER No. 24.
BY LIEUT. COL. J. H. P. MORRELL M.V.O.
COMMANDING 9th BATTN. MANCHESTER REGT.

Reference Sheet 1/100,000 NAMUR.

MARCH TO THE RHINE.

1. In accordance with the terms of the Armistice, occupied portions of FRANCE, BELGIUM and LUXEMBURG are to be evacuated by the enemy by November 26th.
    A further withdrawal to East of Rhine is to take place at a later date.

2. The advance of the Allied Forces is to commence on November 17th.

3. 66th Division is to lead the advance on the Right of the British Army. The 169 French Division will be on its Right, and 1st (British) Division on its Left.
    66th Division is to be preceded by 2nd Cavalry Division which will cover the front of the Fourth Army.
    32nd Division is to follow 66th Division one days march in rear.

4. Divisional boundary to the MEUSE is to be as follows:-
    Northern Boundary.- L'ECREVISSE (excl) -FRASIES (excl) - SIVRY STATION (incl)- RENLIES - SILENRIEUX - FONTAINE - FLORENNES - JUSAINE (all excl) - ROSEE (incl) - ROSEE-DINANT Rd. (excl)

    Southern Boundary. EPPESAUVAGE (incl) - through DE of FORET DE RANCE - Railway Crossing ¼ inch S. of C of CERFONTAINE - SAMARE (excl) - VILLERS LE GAMBON. (incl)- SURICE (incl) - Road junction ⅜ inch W. of H of HEER.

5. Preliminary Moves.

    a. On November 18th the 1st Division is to take over the portion of the front from FRASIES - BOIS DE BEAURIEUX - L' ECREVISSE (all inclusive to 1st Division)
    b. By 1900 hours November 16th Battalion will be disposed as in Appendix A.

6. On November 18th the Division is to advance in Brigade Groups with 199th Infantry Brigade Group leading along the road RANCE - FROID CHAPELLE - CERFONTAINE - PHILLIPEVILLE - ROSEE. Should the roads be sufficiently good it is intended that the march on the 18th should be on the line L;EAU D' HEURE.

7. Military precautions will be observed on the line of march as follows:-
    i. When the 199th Infantry Brigade Group is leading the leading Battalion will detail an escort and covering party of 2 Coys (under 2nd in Command of Battn.) to accompany the billeting and working parties which will be moving a day in advance of the Main Body of the Division.
        Working parties will consist of:-
            1 Field Coy R.E.
            1 Section Tunnelling Coy R.E.
            Proportion of Pioneer Battn.
        and additional working parties are to be held in readiness at the head of Brigade Group in case they should be required.
    ii. When the Brigade is advancing it will march with an Advance Guard of 1 Battalion (less 2 Coys) including 1 Batty. R.F.A.
    iii. In billets the leading Battalion will picquet the roads leading from front and flanks to their billets.

8. a. Subject to the above, the comfort of the troops will be the principal object in the conduct of the march.
   Bands will be, and Colours may be, taken on the march.
   b. Coy Commanders will be responsible that the strictest march discipline is maintained.
   c. DRESS. Full Marching Order, 1 blanket and leather in lieu of greatcoat; helmet worn in lieu of cap; 70 rounds S.A.A. carried by each man in lieu of 120 rounds.
   Coys will send to Q.M. Stores, vide orders issued, 50 rounds S.A.A. per man.

(signature)
Captain and Adjutant.
9th Battn. Manchester Regt.

APPENDIX A.

COMPOSITION OF BATTALION BY 1800 hours November 10th.

Battn H.Q., "A", "B", "D" Coy   In present location.
"C" Coy.   Take over posts held by 5th Conn R;grs.
                                  by 1000 hours to-day.

Appendix No 7.

Operation Order No 25

SECRET   Copy No....

OPERATION ORDER — NUMBER 25
BY LIEUT COLONEL J. F. B. MORRELL MVO
COMMANDING 9th Battalion MANCHESTER REGIMENT

17. 11. 18

1. The Battalion will move to-morrow 18th instant to CERFONTAINE

2. Starting Point — "B" Coy Headquarters.

3. Head of Battalion to be at Starting Point at 0630 hrs in following order H.Q. B, Band, D. A. C. Coys.

4. DRESS — Marching Order. Steel Helmets to be worn, Gas Helmets resting on top of packs. Blanket, jerkin and canteen to be carried inside and watershest rubber sheet outside pack. Greatcoat will be carried on G. S. wagon allotted to companies.

5. ROUTINE — REVEILLE 0430 hrs.   BREAKFAST 0515 hrs
   LOADING OF WAGONS 0545 hrs.
   DINNER ON COMPLETION OF MARCH

6. Orders for Transport as issued in Instructions for March to the RHINE.

7. 1 N.C.O., with bicycles, per company H.Q. and Transport to report to 2/Lt C.F. GROVES, as billetting party at head of column at Starting Point at 0630 hrs.

8. 1 N.C.O. and 3 O.R. per company under an officer of rear coy. to march in rear of Transport, to collect stragglers and to take charge of company wagons on arrival at destination.

9. Marching Out States to be sent to Battalion Orderly Room by 0530 hrs. Marching In States, showing number of men who have fallen out during March, to be rendered immediately on arrival at destination.

10. 10 yards intervals will be maintained between companies on line of march.

L A Turvey

Capt. and Adjt.,
9th Battalion Manchester Regiment.

Distribution — Normal.

Appendix No 8

Special Order by Maj. Gen. H.K. BETHELL.
C.M.G. D.S.O.

SPECIAL ORDER.

66th Division, I take this opportunity, on the eve of our march to the Rhine, to thank every one of you, Officer, N.C.O. and man, for your hard work during the past months, and for the cheerful, determined spirit in which you have tackled and dealt with any and all situations.

It is entirely owing to this spirit, combined with hard work, that the Division has been uniformly successful, whether in exterminating the malaria and fitting itself for battle, or in exterminating the enemy in battle itself.

It is this spirit to which the word "impossible" is unknown, that has enabled the Division to make a name for itself in the British Army in so short a time. Above all, it is this spirit which will stand you in most stead throughout your lives, however employed.

Fortunate in great opportunities and weather, the Division has exploited both to the full. To it fell the honour of retaking Le Cateau. Forming part of the Fourth Army Advanced Guard, it was the last Division of this Army to be in action with the enemy. At 11.00, 11th November, 1918, on the termination of hostilities, it was holding the Fourth Army front, and in close touch with the enemy. It is now about to advance to the Rhine on the right of the British Army.

South Africans, Irishmen and Englishmen, you have proved yourselves all to be magnificent infantry.

Engineers and Pioneers, you have shown yourselves to be of the same metal as your infantry.

Artillery, you have been away from us for a long time, but you returned with excellent reports from the Corps and Division with whom you had been serving and where you had well upheld the name of the Division.

Signal Service, you have steadily improved throughout the year, and your work in the late fighting was splendid. The task of keeping communication during the latter stages was one of extraordinary difficulty and could only have been coped with as successfully as it was by indefatigable efforts on the parts of all ranks of your Company.

Train and M.T., with you as with the infantry, there has been no "impossible." Your untiring efforts have contributed in no small way to success, and have been greatly appreciated by the troops.

Medical Services, in and out of battle, your work has been consistently excellent. The very low sick wastage in the Division is largely the result of your continuous efforts.

Machine Gun Battalion, though not long with the Division, your work up to date, in or out of action, confirms the very good report with which you came to us.

Commanders and Staffs, you have had a most difficult and anxious time. The cheerful wholehearted way in which you tackled every new combination, whether of training Cadres and American Divisions, or later of Battalions, making a success of all, foretold the results you have now obtained.

The Division has now been selected as one of those Divisions to carry out the march to the Rhine preparatory to the occupation of German territory in accordance with the terms of the Armistice.

Remember that we are on the right of the British line and about to pass through country where British troops have never been seen. French troops are on our right, the 1st Division is on our left. By our appearance and conduct the Imperial Army will be judged for years to come.

I expect every one of you in the same cheeful determined spirit, by the excellence of your discipline and turnout, and by your soldierly behaviour, to maintain the name of the 66th Division as high in peace as you have set it in war.

H. K. BETHELL, *Major-General,*
Commanding 66th Division.

Divisional Headquarters,
17th November, 1918.

Field Survey Bn., R.E. 4490—1000—20-11-18.

Appendix No 9.

Operation Order No 27

SECRET   Copy No. 2

OPERATION ORDER No. 27.
BY LIEUT.COL. J.P.R. MORRELL M.V.O.
COMMANDING 9th BATTN. MANCHESTER REGT.

23/11/18.

Reference Map NAMUR S. 1/100,000.

1. The Battn. will move tomorrow the 24th inst to MORVILLE.
   Approximate distance of march- 10 MILES.

2. Head of Battn. will leave Battn. H.Q. at 0705 hours and Coys will
   join column as it passes Coy Billets in following order:
   Band, H.Q., "A", "B", "C", "D", Coys.

3. ROUTINE. REVEILLE 0500 hours, KITS AND GREATCOATS LOADED BY 0530.
   BREAKFAST 0600 hrs. DINNERS AT HALT ABOUT MIDDAY.
   Sick Parade will be held tonight at 1630 hours.

4. The Battn. will march in THREES. Distances as laid down in
(i) F.S. Pocket Book, page 33, will be maintained.
    On the line of march compliments will only be paid to:
    (a) Commander-in-Chief on all occasions.
    (b) Army, Corps, and Divisional Commanders, once (the first time
        of passing) daily unless the Army, Corps or Divisional
        Commander passes in a car when compliments will NOT be paid.
    (c) Guards.
    (d) Commanding Officers of units as their troops march into
        billets.
(ii) Officers will salute individually in all cases when passing
     General Officers.
(iii) In future during the march to the RHINE, men will be allowed
      to smoke AFTER the first halt, and not at halts only as previously
      ordered.

5. Billetting party will assemble at B.O.R. at 0615 hours under
   2/Lieut. C.F. GROVES.

6. TRANSPORT.   Coy limbers and mules will move behind Coys.
   The remainder of Transport will move in rear of Battn. under
   orders of Transport Officer.
   Coys will detail 1 N.C.O. and 2 men each to report to O.C. "B" Coy
   who will detail an Officer to take charge of party.
   This party will march in rear of Transport to collect stragglers
   and assist Transport when necessary.

7. Marching Out States will be rendered to B.O.R. by 0800 hours.
   Marching In States, showing number of Men who have fallen out,
   immediately on arrival at new destination.

                                              L A Tuey
                                              Captain and Adjutant.
                                              9th Battn. Manchester Regt.

Distribution - Normal.

CONFIDENTIAL

WAR DIARY

OF

9½ Bn THE MANCHESTER REGT.

From 1st to 31st December, 1918. (Armistice Period)

Volume No. 4. — No 12

WAR DIARY
INTELLIGENCE SUMMARY.

(Erase heading not required.)

December 1918. 2/7th Br. The Manchester Regt.

Army Form C. 2118.

Place	Date	Hour	Summary of Events and Information	Remarks and references to Appendices
MORVILLE	1-12-18		Capt C.H. GREENWELL and Lieut HOWARTH having reported this arrived 23-11-14 and taken on the effective strength from that date and posted the "B" and "C" Coys respectively. Capt F.A. COWEN T.F. was attached to "A" Coy. Brigade Church Service at CHATEAU 1 mile SOUTH of ANTHÉE (Bde HQ) on 22-11-18. CAPT C.N. GREENWELL taken over command of "C" Coy with effect from 1-12-18. CAPT GOLDSCHMIDT having gone to hospital.	NAMUR 1/100,000
-do-	2-12-18		Physical Training and Arm drill. The Divisional band will play in the aerodrome, MORVILLE tomorrow from 14.30 - 16.00 hours and to "LANCASHIRE LADS" on the 5th at 6 p.m.	
-do-	3-12-18		Physical Training and Battalion Parade given by the Adjutant. The Field Marshall Commander in-Chief under authority delegated by His Majesty The King, awarded decorations as follows to the undermentioned Officers and Other Ranks for gallantry and devotion to duty during the recent operations. (Bar to the Military Cross), Capt F.T. TAYLOR M.C, The Military Cross (Lieut) J.W. BENNETT, D.C.M. No 9648 Sergt G. COOMBES "B" Coy, M.M. No 14572 Sergt A.L. SNOWDEN, "C" Coy. Educational Classes as usual.	
-do-	4-12-18		Battalion started on route march but was forced to return owing to bad weather. Arm drill and Saluting in billets were carried out instead. Inoculation commenced.	
-do-	5-12-18		Battalion did the route march that was attempted yesterday.	
-do-	6-12-18		Brigade Ceremonial drill on aerodrome ground.	
-do-	7-12-18		Inspection of billets by C.O. followed by Coy Kit inspection.	
-do-	8-12-18		Voluntary Church Service as usual. Lieut P.R.E. SAEPPARD R.A.M.C lectured to the Battalion in theatre at 11.45 hours. The subject was - "SOUTH AFRICA", the lecture was most interesting as well as amusing. The men quite enjoyed it.	
-do-	9-12-18		Physical training and arm drill. "B" Coy (Capt F.T. TAYLOR M.C) was suddenly sent about 15 P.D.T. Prisoners of War E.C. to ANDENNES to be available to quell civil disturbances. This town, if not more, is to be the X Corps - the X Corps. The Coy moved on the 8-12-18.	

Army Form C. 2118.

WAR DIARY
INTELLIGENCE SUMMARY.

(Erase heading not required.)

December 1918   2/6 Bn The Manchester Regt.

Place	Date	Hour	Summary of Events and Information	Remarks and references to Appendices
MORVILLE	10-12-18		R.S.M. parade, ceremonial. M.O's inspection on Coy billets, lecture by M.O. on threats on Venereal Disease. B.O.C. 199th Bde inspected Battalion Transport. The routine administration of Quinine may now be discontinued. Where men have relapses the quinine treatment will again be commenced. Fresh money will be used until further orders are issued.	O.C. 6th Bn NAMUR 8. 11,000,000 MARCHE 9. LIEGE 7. September 10.
"	11-12-18		Company parades. Operation Order No 28 (Appendix No) issued. The Battalion will move on the 13th, 14th and 15th December to DINANT, HAMOIS, and HUY. Operational dress as usual.	
"	12-12-18		Parades as for yesterday.	
"	13-12-18		Battalion marched according to programme to DINANT and were in billets by 12.30 hours.	
DINANT	14-12-18		Battalion marched to HAMOIS where it arrived and was billeted by 14.30 hours, the march was very long and the route was very hilly.	
HAMOIS				
HUY	15-12-18		The Battalion moved off at 11 hours, before setting off to column might be, after the main CINEY-LANDENNE road, when the Commander in Chief was to pass. The Battalion halted from 10.50 hrs to 12.00 hours for dinner, after which marched into HUY at 14.30 hours very well and with every appearance of being very fresh. 8 grains of quinine were given to every man in the evening.	
"	16-12-18		Cleaning of equipment and clothing. Games canceling must be attached unto BELGIUM.	
"	17-12-18		Parade 9.30-10.00 hrs Coy inspection and handling arms. 10.00-12.30 hrs cleaning up. T.A.B. 1x2 inoculation for all ranks not already done.	

Army Form C. 2118.

WAR DIARY
or
INTELLIGENCE SUMMARY.
(Erase heading not required.)

Army Form C. 2118.

Place	Date	Hour	Summary of Events and Information	Remarks and references to Appendices
HUY.	18-12-18		Parades 1/2 hour Physical training and two hours sleeping billets and surroundings. Educational Classes will not be continued until further orders. HUY is one of the oldest towns in BELGIUM though small. The houses are very good. "A" and "D" Coys are billeted in a large disused factory, "B" Coy in what is a picture gallery and "D" Coy is split up in two empty houses. H.Q (Coy) Band Drums and most of the transport are in the GENDARMERIE, a very fine building where every man has a bed and where the transport horses still sit stables. Eatteries, washing troughs and coatcranes are on hand for all companies and Company rifles also have Serbian disinfector trucks. A "Nursing Society" building has been taken over and when ready will be used as a school for part of the day and as an institute (writing room or being) in the afternoons. (Officers) Messes by Companies are in private houses and the Battalion is more comfortable than it has been for ages. Billets by G.O.C. Brigade. The 664 Divisions is not started to the Inspection. General proceeding by Etain evages. Leave will do so direct to NAMUR by train leaving HUY at 1:55. Four Etain evages in the town are open to troops as under. 12.00 - 14.00 hrs and 18.00 - 21.00 hrs. Examination and stripping of rifles commences today. Men are allowed into the town properly dressed after 14.00 hrs.	HUY/1:50,000 LIEGE 1 1:100,000
	20 Dec 18		Parades 1/2 hour Physical Training two hours cleaning of billets and surroundings	

Army Form C. 2118.

WAR DIARY
or
INTELLIGENCE SUMMARY
(Erase heading not required.)

Regt: 2/6th The Manchester Regt
December 1918

Place	Date	Hour	Summary of Events and Information	Remarks and references to Appendices
HUY	21-12-18		Work and parades as usual. Extract from Battalion Orders of 19-12-18. "Under authority delegated by His Majesty the King, the Field Marshal Commanding-in-Chief has made the following grants for gallantry during recent operations.— D.S.O. Bt Major (T/Lieut Col) J.F.B. MORRELL M.V.O R. LANC. REGT att MANCHESTER REGT." Retaining hours are altered to 10.30–13.30 hrs and 17.30–21.00 hrs. Inter platoon football competition is in progress.	Perhaps LIEGE 1:100,000
"	22-12-18		Voluntary Church Services in the Theatre and Battalion School. A very good lecture on "Subjects from Dickens" was given to the troops in the theatre.	
"	23-12-18		Course of training has commenced. Rolls of men by Dispersal Stations and Areas are being called for with a view to Demobilisation.	Appendix 2
"	24-12-18		Training as per programme. Barrack rooms and dining rooms are being decorated for tomorrow.	Appendix no 2
"	25-12-18		Brigade Church Service in Brigade Theatre at 10.00 hours. The mens dinner were served at 13.30 hours. The meal consisted of Turkey, a proportion of Geese, full meat ration, extra vegetables, ration bought from Regtl funds, two good hams per Coy, plum pudding, and plenty of Beer. 6 to 4 cigarettes per man were supplied. The Commanding Officer directed dinner and everyone seemed perfectly satisfied.	
"	26-12-18		Boxing Day was observed as a holiday.	
"	27-12-18		Routine. Training and Education carried on as per programme issued. Riding Classes for Officers will be continued twice weekly.	

Army Form C. 2118.

WAR DIARY

INTELLIGENCE SUMMARY. 9th Bn The Manchester Regt

(Erase heading not required.)

December 1918

Place	Date	Hour	Summary of Events and Information	Remarks and references to Appendices
HUY	28-12-18		Routine, Training and Education as per programme.	Ref. Maps LIEGE Y. 1:100,000
"	29-12-18		Brigade Church Service in Brigade Theatre.	
"	30-12-18		Training and Education as per programme.	
"	31-12-18		Training steps as before. The introduction of two newspapers of German origin into Belgium is prohibited. The health of the troops is excellent. The effective strength of the Battalion is 42 Officers and 763 other ranks. Reinforcements during month 12 Officers & 65 O.R. Men demobilised during month 156 O.R.	
	1-1-19			

H.B. Morrell. Lieut Col
Cmdg 9th Bn The Manchester Regt

Appendix No 1

Operation Order No 28

SECRET

OPERATION ORDER NUMBER
BY LIEUT COLONEL J. F. B. MORRELL M.V.C.
COMMANDING 9th BATTALION MANCHESTER REGIMENT

Copy No. 3

11.12.18.

Reference Maps, NAMUR 8. MARCHE 9, LIEGE 7. 1/100,000

1. The Battalion will move on the 13th 14th and 15th December in accordance with attached table.

2. On 15th December there will be a mid-day halt from 1150 - 1300 hrs On 13th and 14th Decr. there will be no mid-day halt.

3.
   a. Billeting Party for Dec 13th, consisting of 2/Lt C HILL MC and 1 NCO per Coy. 1 H.Q. and 1 Tpt, will assemble at B.O.R. at 0930 hrs on the 12th instant, with bicycles. This party will move off to meet the Staff Capt. at Town Major's Office, DINANT at 1100 hrs. Rations for the 13th instant to be taken.
   b. Billeting Party for 14th Dec. will assemble that day at B.O.R. at 0830 hrs. Party will consist of Major R.M.L. Scott M C 1 NCO per Coy, H.Q., TPT and 544 Coy ASC. Brigade will not provide any billets and all arrangements for billeting the Battalion and 544 Coy. ASC. will be under Major SCOTT.

4.
   a. First Line Transport will move with the Battalion as ordered in "MARCH TO RHINE"
   b. Baggage wagons will report to Battalion by midday 12th Dec. and remain until conclusion of the march when they will rejoin the 544 Coy, ASC.
   c. Allotment of lorries and G S Wagons to companies will be notified later.

5. DRESS - Full Marching Order - 1 Blanket in pack. Steel Helmet to be worn and gas helmet slung.
   Greatcoats to be carried on transport allotted to companies

6. The Corps Commander has ordered
   a. Men walking out after arrival in billets must be properly dressed with belts.
   b. If horses have to be picketed out on grassland, care to be taken that as small a space is taken up as possible, and that in no case are they to be picketed where they can damage trees

7. Watches will be synchronised daily by the Signal Officer.

8. Each Coy. and Headquarters will detail daily on the march a party of 1 NCO and 3 O.R. to report to O C Coy in rear. This party is required to march in rear of the Transport to assist any Transport in difficulties and to collect stragglers.
O.C. Rear Coy. will detail an officer
to take charge of this party

L. A. Turney

Capt. and Adjt.,
9th Battalion Manchester Regiment

Distribution - Normal
plus 544 Coy. A.S.C.
Billeting Officers.

MARCH TABLE TO ACCOMPANY OPERATION ORDER NUMBER 3

DATE.	ORDER OF COMPANIES.	FROM	TO	ROUTE	STARTING POINT	TIME TO PASS S.P.
13. 12. 18	Band, H.Q., "C" Coy. Drums "A", "D" Coys Transport. Company markers to report to R.SM. at AERODROME at 0825 hours. Companies to march on markers by 0830 hours.	MORVILLE	DINANT	ANTHEE ONHAYE	Parade Ground Aerodrome	0835 hrs
14. 12. 18	Drums H.Q. "A" Coy. Band, "D" "C" Coys Transport.	DINANT	HAMOIS	CINEY CINEY — HAVALANGE Rd.	to be notified later	
15. 12. 18	Band, H.Q. "D" Coy Drums "C" "A" Coys Transport	HAMOIS	HUY	SCHALTIN OHEY PERWEZ	— do —	

Appendix No 2.

Programme of Training

PROGRAMME OF TRAINING.

WEEK ENDING SATURDAY DECEMBER 28th 1918.

CLASS I

DAY.	0700-0730	0900 - 1000	1000 - 1100	1100 - 1130	1145 - 1230.
MONDAY DEC. 23rd.	Roll Call Reading of Orders & Run.	Squadding & making of Nominal Rolls by Instructors.	Squad Drill with arms by numbers. ½ hour. Saluting.	Musketry	Handling of Arms. Musketry.
TUESDAY DEC. 24th.	do.	P.T.	Handling of Arms & Drill.	Lecture on Interior Economy & Cleanliness.	Platoon Drill with Platoon.
WEDNESDAY DEC. 25th	CHRISTMAS DAY		CHURCH PARADE.		
THURSDAY DEC. 26th	Roll Call Reading of Orders & ½hr Run.	Bayonet Training.	Squad Drill ½ hour Saluting.	Musketry.	Drill & Handling of Arms. Musketry.
FRIDAY DEC. 27th	do.	P.T.	Handling of Arms. Guard Mounting.	Lecture on Cleaning of Equipment & Sanitation.	Drill with Platoon.
SATURDAY DEC. 28th	do. without run.	B.F.	Inspection of billets by C.O. Squad Drill & Saluting.	Musketry	Handling of arms and Drill with Coy.

N.B. The 0700 - 0730 and 1145 - 1230 parades are done with their own Company and Platoons.

Marked Men's Drill   1400 - 1500 hours.

Inspection of Coy Billets by O.C. Coys at 0930 hours.

CLASS II.

DAY	0700 – 0730	0900 – 1000	1000 – 1100	1100 – 1130	1145 – 1230
MONDAY DEC. 23rd.	Roll Call. Reading of Orders & Run.	P.T. under Instructors.	Handling of Arms under Instrs. & Saluting.	Musketry.	Handling of Arms with Coy.
TUESDAY DEC. 24th	do.	B.F. under Instr.	L.G. Training & R.G. do. under Instr.	Lecture on Interior Economy & Cleanliness.	Platoon Drill with Platoon.
WED. DEC. 25th	CHRISTMAS DAY		CHURCH PARADE.		
THURSDAY. DEC. 26th.	Roll Call Reading of Orders & ¼ hr Run.	P.T. under Instr.	Handling of Arms & Guard Mounting under Instr.	Lecture on Cleaning of Equipment & Sanitation.	Drill & Handling of Arms with Coy.
FRIDAY DEC. 27th.	do.	B.F. under Instr.	L.G. Train. R.G. do. under Instr.	MUSKETRY.	Drill with Platoon.
SATURDAY DEC. 28th.	do. without run.	P.T.	Inspection of Billets by C.O. Handling of Arms & Saluting.	Muskretry	Handling of Arms with Coy.

CLASS III.

	0700 – 0730	0900 – 0930	1100 – 1130	1145 – 1230
MONDAY DEC. 23rd.	Roll Call Reading of Orders & ¼ hr Run.	P.T.	Musketry	Handling of Arms with Coy.
TUESDAY DEC. 24th	do.	B.T.	Lecture on Interior Economy & Cleanliness	Drill with Platoons
WEDNESDAY DEC. 25th	CHRISTMAS DAY		CHURCH PARADE.	
THURSDAY DEC 26th.	Roll Call Reading of Orders & Run.	P.T.	L.G. Training.	Handling of Arms & Drill with Coy.
FRIDAY DEC. 27th.	do.	B.T.	Lecture on Cleaning equipment & Sanitation.	Drill with Platoons.
SATURDAY DEC. 28th.	do without run.	Cleaning of Billets.	Inspection of Billets by C.O. 1000 hrs.	Handling of Arms & Drill with Coy.

CLASS IV.

DAY.	0700 - 0730	0900 - 1000	1000 - 1100	1100 - 1130	1145 - 1230
MONDAY DEC 23rd	Roll Call. Reading of Orders ¼ hr Run.	Squad Drill Handling of Arms under R.S.M.	Musketry under Sgt Hodson	Lecture on duties of N.C.O.s and bearing towards men by R.S.M.	Handling of Arms with Coy.
TUESDAY. DEC 24th.	do.	Guard Mount. & Ceremonial under T.S.M.	B.T. under Regt. Instr. & Sgt Miles.	Lecture on Interior Economy & Cleanliness.	Drill with Platoon.
WEDNESDAY. DEC 25th	CHRISTMAS DAY.		CHURCH PARADE.		
THURSDAY DEC 26th.	Roll Call. Reading of Orders & Run.	Squad Drill & Handling of Arms under R.S.M.	B.T. under Regt. Instr & Sgt Miles.	Lecture on Guides & Markers. Ceremonial under R.S.M.	Handling of Arms & Drill with Coy.
FRIDAY DEC. 27th.	do.	Guard Mount. & Ceremonial under R.S.M.	Musketry under Sgt Hodson.	Lecture on Cleaning Equip. & Sanitation.	Drill with Platoon.
SATURDAY. DEC. 28th.	do. withour run.	Supervision of cleaning of billets.	Inspection of billets by C.O.	L.G. Train. under Sgt Brookes.	Handling of Arms and Drill with Coy.

CONFIDENTIAL.

9/N 23

WAR DIARY

of

9TH BN. THE MANCHESTER REGT.

From 1st to 31st January 1919 (ARMISTICE PERIOD)

VOLUME No 5 — No 1.

Army Form C. 2118.

WAR DIARY
or
INTELLIGENCE SUMMARY.
(Erase heading not required.)

2nd Batt. Lanchester Regt. January 1919

Instructions regarding War Diaries and Intelligence Summaries are contained in F.S. Regs., Part II. and the Staff Manual respectively. Title pages will be prepared in manuscript.

Place	Date	Hour	Summary of Events and Information	Remarks and references to Appendices
HUY	1-1-19		Training carried out as per programme.	Map that he got 1/100,000
	2-1-19		Training carried out as per programme.	
	3-1-19		Training as per programme. Major R.M.C. Pratt M.C. handed over duties of C.R.S. and Regimental Infant Officer to Capt. C.D. Walker O.B.E.	
	4-1-19		Training as per programme. O.B.E.	
	5-1-19		Brigade Church Service was held in the Hall. The men were sent home for demobilization.	
	6-1-19		Training and Education was carried out as per programme. The usual eighty attiring the programme of last week.	
	7-1-19		Training and Education as per programme. 2 time serving soldiers were sent home for leave prior to rejoining. C.R.S.	
	8-1-19		Battalion Route March. Education cancelled owing to Route March. C.R.S.	
	9-1-19		Training and Education as per programme. The X Corps Commander visited the Battalion. The No 10 Special parade. 10 or of Group 43 (Educational) were sent away.	
	10-1-19		Training and Education as per programme. 9 miners and demobilized were sent away. The Recruits and Junior N.C.O.'s class passed before the Commanding Officer for preliminary posting) out late O.B.	
	11-1-19		Training and Education as per programme. 2 demobilizes were sent home.	
	12-1-19		Brigade Church Service in the Theatre. C.R.S.	
	13-1-19		Training as per revised programme. Groups 1,2, 3, 10, 30, 33, 35) were sent away. The G.O.C. Division inspects the Garrison of the Battalion at 1-00 hours. The transport was well turned out and on pass from the General. C.R.S.	
	14-1-19		Training and Education as per programme. Lieut Percival took over the duties of Transport Officer from Lieut E.A. Ralston who proceeded to leave. C.R.S.	

Army Form C. 2118.

WAR DIARY
INTELLIGENCE SUMMARY
(Erase heading not required.)

January 1919   9th Bn. Manchester Regt.

Place	Date	Hour	Summary of Events and Information	Remarks and references to Appendices
HUY	15-1-19		Training and Education as per programme. C.B.	
	16-1-19		Training and Education as per programme. 29 O.R. were sent away for demobilisation. The second Board out here was held to to R Recruits which resulted in 2/Lt ---- & 83 broing at B.A.R.	
	17-1-19		Training and Education as per programme.— The Company Offrs Lieut Cols J.F.B. Morrell D.S.O. M.V.O. Corps comdg and the Brigade. Brig Gen G.C. Williams therewof, on leave. Capt H.T. Taylor took over/ comnd of the Battalion. A new programme of Training in view owing to companies being so small, average strength per company 95. (See appendix 1) C.B.	Appendix I
	18-1-19 20-1-19 21-1-19		Brigade Church service in Brigade Theatre. C.B. Education and Training as per programme C.B. Training and Education as per programme. The Army Brigadier General Officer Comdg Lt. R.M. N.Q. interviewed D Company. All demobilising who fifteen men. Batalion Route March about 10 miles. Work was carried out in relief by parties	
	22-1-19		of the companies on the Rifle Range. C.B.	
	23-1-19		Work, training and Education was carried out as per programme. A Lecture to Officers by Major Bertrand Smith, on the Naval Raid to ZEEBRUGGE was informally arranged. The Transport section carried out a Route March C.B.	
	24-1-19		Training, Work + Education was carried out as per programme. All ranks Officer Others attended a Parade to Listen to the presentation by His Excellency Show having fallen there were no visits to Companies for Inspn. the work that in the event of a heavy fall, C.B.	
	25-1-19		Training and Education were carried out. It was certain Classes (enumerated) would be stopped owing to Orders were issued that Certain Classes (enumerated) would be stopped owing to	

Army Form C. 2118.

WAR DIARY
or
INTELLIGENCE SUMMARY
(Erase heading not required.)

9th Batt. Manchester Regt.

January 1919

Place	Date	Hour	Summary of Events and Information	Remarks and references to Appendices
HUY	26-1-19		Sunday Service as the previous Sunday. C.D.R.	Appendix 1. Appendix 2.
	27-1-19		Training was carried out as per new programme (see appendix No 2) but Educational Classes as per programme. C.D.R following extracts was published in Order from the LONDON GAZETTE No 31197 of 6-1-19. That T/M BENNETT to be T/Lt. 30-11-18 and T/2/Lt. (A/Capt.) F RUDDY to be T/Lt. 30-11-18. C.D.R.	
	28-1-19		Training, work and Education as per programme. C.D.R.	
	29-1-19		Battalion carried out a Route march of about 10 miles. Order issued on the 21st visit cancelling demobilization is cancelled. C.D.R.	
	30-1-19		Training, work and Education as per programme. C.D.R.	
	31-1-19		Educational Classes cancelled owing to low attendance. Training and work as per programme. A Route march was carried out by the Transport Section. Distance about 12 miles. C.D.R.	
			The health of the Troops has been excellent during the month. Effective Strength of the Battalion is 27 Officers and 528 Other ranks. Total demobilization during month 9 Officers 201 Other ranks. C.D.R.	

1-2-19.

R.H. Duke, Major
Comdg 9th Bn. The Manchester Regt.

Appendix No 1.

Programme of Training

9th BATTALION MANCHESTER REGIMENT.

PROGRAMME OF TRAINING   W.E. 25/1/19.

DAY.	0700 – 0730	0900 – 0930	1030 – 11.30	11.45 – 1330
FRIDAY, JAN 17th	Roll Call. Reading of Orders & Run.	Inspection. P.T.	L.G. Cleaning Name of parts & Description.	Ceremonial. Sizing. Handling of Arms on the move.
SATURDAY, JAN 18th.	do. without run.	Cleaning of billets.	Inspection of stables by G.O.C.	Ceremonial.
MONDAY, JAN 20th.	Roll Call. Reading of Orders & Run.	Inspection. P.T.	L.G. cleaning & Mech.	Ceremonial.
TUESDAY, JAN 21st.	do.	Inspection. B.T.	L.G. Mech. & Gun Drill.	Ceremonial Drill as Sentries.
WEDNESDAY, JAN 22nd.	do.	BATTALION ROUTE MARCH.		
THURSDAY, JAN 23rd.	do.	Inspection. P.T.	L.G. Mech. & Gun Drill.	Ceremonial.
FRIDAY, JAN 24th.	do.	Inspection. B.T.	L.G. Stoppages.	Practice Presentation of Colours. Ceremonial.
SATURDAY, JAN 25th.	do. without run.	Cleaning of Billets.	Inspection of billets by C.O.	Ceremonial.

Appendix No 2.

Programme of Training

TRAINING PROGRAMME. WEEK ENDING 1/2/18.

	0700 - 0730	0900 - 0930	1030 - 1130	1145 - 130
MONDAY. JAN 27th.	Roll Call. Reading of Orders & Run.	Inspection. P.T.	L.G. Descript. & Mech.	Ceremonial. Slow March.
TUESDAY. JAN 28th.	do.	Inspection. P.T.	L.G. Stoppages.	Ceremonial. Handling of Arms on the move
WEDNESDAY. JAN 29th.	do.	Battalion Route March.		
THURSDAY. JAN. 30th.	do.	Inspection. P.T.	L.G. Gun Drill (2 Teams) Mech.	Ceremonial Drill as Sentries.
FRIDAY. JAN 31st.	do.	Inspection. P.T.	L.G. Drill (2 teams) Stoppages.	Ceremonial. Guard Mounting.
SATURDAY. FEB. 1st.	do. without run.	Cleaning of billets.	Inspection of billets by C.O.	Ceremonial.

CONFIDENTIAL

WAR DIARY

OF

THE MANCHESTER REGT.

9TH Bn

From 1st to 28th FEBRUARY 1919 (ARMISTICE PERIOD)

VOLUME 5 No 2.

Army Form C. 2118.

WAR DIARY
or
INTELLIGENCE SUMMARY

(Erase heading not required.)

February 1919   9th Bn. The Connaught Rangers

Place	Date	Hour	Summary of Events and Information	Remarks and references to Appendices
HUY	1-2-19		Cleaning of billets. Inspection of billets by C.O. Ceremonial.	
-do-	2-2-19		Brigade Church Services as usual. 19 O.R. and 9 O.R. demobilised 1-2-19 and 2-2-19 respectively. Strength 100,000	
-do-	3-2-19.		Rehearsal of Presentation of Colours to the 6th Bn. CONNAUGHT RANGERS, the Pipes & Drums, Band, ENVERARD, carried on the hang and the Submarines.	Appendix No. 1.
-do-	4-2-19.		Training as per programme (Appendix No. 1) started	
-do-	5-2-19		Training as above.	
-do-	6-2-19		Training as above.	
-do-	7-2-19		Training as above.	
-do-	8-2-19.		Cleaning and Inspection of billets. Ceremonial.	
-do-	9-2-19		Brigade Church Services as usual. "A" and "D" Coys are now Nos 1 Coy and "B" & "C" Coys No 2 Coy.	
-do-	10-2-19		Training as per programme (Appendix No. 2) started. Brigade Boxing Competition.	Appendix No. 2.
-do-	11-2-19		Training as per programme. Tomorrow's route march will not take place, training will be carried out as for Friday 14th inst. The C.O. regrets to announce the death of Pte in the 50th CCS No 5965 Pte J HADFIELD "D" Coy on 9-2-19.	
-do-	12-2-19		Training as for 14th inst. or programme	
-do-	13-2-19.		Operation Order No 29 (Appendix No 3) issued. Battalion will move to SEILLES tomorrow.	Appendix No 3.
-do-	14-2-19		The Battalion paraded at 10.50 hrs and marched to SEILLES and was in billets by 13.30 hrs.	

Army Form C. 2118.

WAR DIARY
INTELLIGENCE SUMMARY.
(Erase heading not required.)

February 1919 of 1/8 Bn The Manchester Regt

Place	Date	Hour	Summary of Events and Information	Remarks and references to Appendices
SEILLES	15-2-19		Routine as usual. Inspection of arms and cleaning of billets. The undermentioned vehicles drawn by 6 horse Artillery horses on loan to the Battalion paraded at 0900 hours under Lieut W. TRENGVAN to proceed to the 66th Div. Demobilisation Stores, CINEY. 4 G.S. limbers, 2 Field Kitchens. All Lewis guns and their equipment by the limbers and placed in charge of a guard of 1 NCO and 4 OR which will remain in charge at CINEY.	Ref. Map LIEGE. Y. 1:100,000
-do-	16-2-19		Church Parade Service in HARMONIQUE. All NCOs and men left with the Battalion who are to form the Cadre will be accommodated in its accustomed Coys with the exception of HQ Coy and Transport will be used as a dump and repository. The "CIRCLE PHILHARMONIQUE." The latter will be used as a dump and repository. HQ Coy will remain in their present billet but will have their quack in the dining Hall. Amongst OR mentioned above will be formed into 1 Coy of 4 platoons under the command of Capt F. RUDDY M.C. D.C.M. No.1 platoon composed of HQ & Batn CADRE under Lieut J.W. BENNETT M.C. Nos 2.3+4 platoons NCOs and men of Jan 1916 and after who are returned made Lieut J.W. DAKIN, 2nd Lieut J.M. RYAN 2nd Lieut W.F. HOWARTH and A. COLLINS D.C.M Lieut N. BANKS - C.S.M. C.S.M. MUNCASTER R.J., C.Q.M.S. - C.Q.M.S. DOBSON D. The following Coy employ will be found by the Coys: 3 cooks for Coy B, 1 cook for Transport 4 sanitary men, 1 Club painters, 1 sanitary man for Transport 4 orderly men, 1 Coy Clerk, 1 Officers Mess cook, 1 Officers mess waiter. Above arrangements came into force with effect 15-2-19. Lieut S.E. SWINNELL reported for duty to precautionary camp.	
-do-	17-2-19		Routine as before. Reveille 06:30 hrs. Roll call 07:15 hrs Breakfast 08:00 hrs. Drill parade 0900-1000 hrs Dinner 1100-1200 hrs Supper 18:00 hrs Inspector of billets and Coy PT or RF 0900-1000 hrs Orderly Room 16:00 hrs Last post 21:30 hrs Lights out 22:00 Inspector of billets by Coy in turn by Teas 16:30 First post 21:00 hrs. C.C.S. No 5731 Pte W. GILMORE "D" Coy on 9-2-19 140 R demobilised whilst on leave are struck off the effective strength.	

Army Form C. 2118.

WAR DIARY
INTELLIGENCE SUMMARY
(Erase heading not required.)

9th Bn The Monmouth Regt

February 1919.

Place	Date	Hour	Summary of Events and Information	Remarks and references to Appendices
SEILLES	18-2-19		The undermentioned Officers having proceeded on demobilization are struck off the effective strength of the Battn stated :- Capt A.K.FOX. M.C. (from 19th Bn Bn H.Q.) 14-2-19, Lieut G.E.CURWEN (from 19th Bn Bn H.Q.) 14-2-19, Capt J.A.F.CALLIS, Capt W.R.BATTY. M.C. 17-2-19, Capt E.W.KERSHAW. 17-2-19, Capt T.A.F.CALLIS, Capt J.P. GOLDSCHMIDT, Lieut E.F. ROBINSON, Lieut W. TREVIVIAN, Lieut W.A. PLUMMER, Lieut N.J. MARGETTS, all on 16-2-19. From 19th 1st Bn H.Q. of demobilization 3 OR 10-2-19, 2 OR 11-2-19, 2 OR 14-2-19. Lieut G.A ROBERTSON having proceeded on demobilization is struck off from today.	Ref Map LIEGE. Y. 1:100,000
-do-	19-2-19		The 6.0 t Coy found no details to the Battalion for three days to meet drafts to station for the concentration camp, and to give concerts in the R&H. amongst in the evening	
-do-	20-2-19		Routine and parades as described on the 17th inst.	
-do-	21-2-19		Routine and parades as above. 1012/149 R.S.M. H.TEMPLE and 3 O.R. having been demobilized are struck off the effective strength with effect from 19-2-19.	
-do-	22-2-19		Inspection of billets by the C.O. The Divisional Commander visited Battn. H.Q.	
-do-	23-2-19		Church Services as usual. Special Influenza precautions are being taken owing to recurrence of epidemic.	
-do-	24-2-19		Inspection of billets. P.T., Bayonet Training etc Recreational Training and Bucket Ball.	
-do-	25-2-19		Recreational Training, Platoon & Coy Drill, Handling of Arms, Guards and Sentries, Musketry,	

Army Form C. 2118.

WAR DIARY

INTELLIGENCE SUMMARY

(Erase heading not required.)

February 1919 9th Bn The Manchester Regt

Place	Date	Hour	Summary of Events and Information	Remarks and references to Appendices
SEILLES	26-2-19		Battalion Route March. In view of Influenza epidemic public places of entertainment are placed out of bounds; including Cinemas will be closed and Church Parade Services held in the open air.	Ref Map 1:100,000
-do-	27-2-19		Recreational Training. Platoon and Company Drill. Handling of Arms Guards and Sentries, Musketry Squires. The undermentioned Officers having proceeded on demobilization from 66% Division are struck off the effective strength of the Battalion with effect from 23-2-19. Capt R.G. THOMAS, Lieut H. JOLLEY.	
-do-	28-2-19		Musketry – team knockout competition, teams 1 Officer or NCO and 4 men selected from platoons, firing at bottle Range 100 yds. no marks submitted. This event did not occur owing to inclement weather. 12 Officers and 304 O.R. were demobilised during the month. Of the Officers, two were from Divisional Headquarters and two from Brigade Headquarters. The health of the troops has been excellent in spite of inclement weather. The effective strength of the Battalion is 20 Officers and 307 O.R.	
	1-3-19			

J.B. Arnold Major
Cmdg 9th Bn Manchester Regt

Appendix No 1.

Programme of Training
Week ending 8-2-19

Army Form C. 2118.

WAR DIARY
or
INTELLIGENCE SUMMARY.

(*Erase heading not required.*)

Instructions regarding War Diaries and Intelligence Summaries are contained in F. S. Regs., Part II. and the Staff Manual respectively. Title pages will be prepared in manuscript.

Place	Date	Hour	Summary of Events and Information	Remarks and references to Appendices

(A8021) Wt. W1771/M2031 750,000 5/17 Sch. 52 Forms/C2118/14 D. D. & L., London, E.C.

AMENDMENT TO PROGRAMME OF TRAINING.

MONDAY. FEB 3rd 1145 – 1230 hours.

Rehearsal of Presentation of Colours to the 5th Bn. Connaught Rangers on HUY Town Football Ground. Battalion will parade at the Chateau Grounds at 1140 hours.

TRAINING PROGRAMME.   Week ending 8/2/19.

Day.	0700 - 0730	0900 - 0930	1030 - 1130	1145 - 1230.
MONDAY. FEB. 3rd.	Roll Call Reading of Orders & Run.	Inspection. P.T.	L.G. Cleaning. Descript. & Mech.	Ceremonial. Battn. Parade.
TUESDAY. FEB 4th.	do.	Inspection. P.T.	Musketry. Fire Pract. Counter Charges.	Ceremonial. Handling of Arms on the move.
WEDNESDAY. FEB 5th.	do.	BATTALION ROUTE MARCH.		
THURSDAY. FEB. 6th.	do.	Inspection. P.T.	L.G. Stoppages. Gun Drill 2 Teams.	Ceremonial. Guard Mounting.
FRIDAY. FEB. 7.	do.	Inspection. P.T.	Musketry. Fire Pract. Bolt Drill Mech. Snap. Shoot. Rapid Fire.	Ceremonial. Drill as Sentries.
SATURDAY. FEB. 8th.	without run.	Cleaning of billets.	Inspection of billets by C.O.	Ceremonial.

See slip attached

Capt CD Wallow

Appendix No 2

Programme of Training
Week ending 15-2-19.

TRAINING PROGRAMME.

Week ending February 15/2/19.

Day.	0700 - 0730	0830 - 1030	1130 - 12 30
MONDAY. FEB. 10.	Roll Call. Reading of Orders and Run.	P.T. Recreational Training.	Coy Drill and Handling of Arms.
TUESDAY. FEB. 11.	do.	No. 1 Coy. P.T. and Basket Ball. No. 2 Coy. all Riflemen firing on ST. LEONARDS RANGE. L.Gns. on L.G. Range RUE LA MOTTE. Firing to commence at 0830 hours.	No. 1 Coy. Company Drill, Handling of Arms. No. 2 Coy as for previous hour.
WEDNESDAY. FEB. 12.	do.	Battalion Route March.	
THURSDAY. FEB. 13.	do.	No. 1 Coy. all riflemen firing on ST LEONARDS Range L.Gns. on L.G. Range, RUE DE LA MOTTE. Firing to commence at 0830 hours. No. 2 Coy. P.T. and Basket Ball.	No. 1 Coy as for previous hour. No. 2 Coy. Coy Drill and Handling of Arms.
FRIDAY. FEB. 14.	do.	No. 1 and 2 Coys.P.T. and Recreational Training.	Platoon Drill and Saluting, and Handling of Arms.
SATURDAY. FEB. 15.	do.	Cleaning of billets and Inspection by C.O.	Coy Drill and Handling of Arms.

Games will be indulged in during the afternoons.

Appendix No 3.

Operation Order No 29.

Army Form C. 2118.

WAR DIARY
or
INTELLIGENCE SUMMARY.
(Erase heading not required.)

Instructions regarding War Diaries and Intelligence Summaries are contained in F. S. Regs., Part II. and the Staff Manual respectively. Title pages will be prepared in manuscript.

Place	Date	Hour	Summary of Events and Information	Remarks and references to Appendices

D. D. & L., London, E.C.
(A8091) Wt. W1771/M2031 750,000 5/17 Sch. 53 Forms/C2118/14

OPERATION ORDER No. 20.
BY LIEUT. COL. J. F. D. MORRELL D.S.O. M.V.C.
COMMANDING 9th BATTALION MANCHESTER REGIMENT.

Copy No 3

13/2/19.

Reference Maps:- LIEGE 1/100.000 MARCHE 1/100.000.

1.   The Battalion is to be demobilised as far as possible and for this purpose will move to SEILLES, to-morrow the 14th inst.
       The Cadre of the Battalion will then move on at a later date to OHEY and to NATOYE to complete demobilization.

2.   The Battalion will parade to-morrow ready to move off at No. 1 Coy billets in the Chateau Grounds at 1000 hours.

3.   DRESS. :- Full marching order, greatcoats in pack, caps will be worn and steel helmets carried on pack. All small kit, mugs etc. are to be packed inside haversack or pack.

4.   Blankets, jerkins, S.B.R.'s, waterproof sheets, and 130 empty palliases per Coy will be collected in dumps at No. 1, 2, and H.Q. Coy Stores, ready for loading on lorries by 0800 hours to-morrow.
       All these articles will be made up in bundles of 10 and clearly labelled.

5.   1 Officer per double Coy and 10 men per double Coy, including Coy storeman, will remain as rear party, and will be responsible for the handing over of various stores to the 1st South African Battn. and loading of lorries, which will be used for two or three journeys if necessary. Men NOT eligible for demobilization are to be left on these parties.

6.   TRANSPORT. : The following is the allotment of transport.
       All horse transport will move with the Battn.
       2 limbers for tools.   3 limbers Battn Reserve S.A.A. (34 boxes
       4 limbers Coy L.G.s and Ammunition.
       1 limber (apportioned as follows) Half for H.Q. L.G.s and half for Orderly Room.
       2 G.S. Wagons for Officers Kit and Officers mess Kits.
       1 lorrie per double Coy and 1 lorry for H.Q. and Q.M.
       Tools, L.G., and ammunition limbers will be loaded up to-day and returned to the Gendarmerie this afternoon.
       Officers kits and Coy Officers Mess Kits will be collected at Q.M. stores by 0900 hours to-morrow.   Signal Stores and Orderly Room Stores (at Gendarmerie) and Orderly Room at 0900 hours and 0915 hours respectively.

7.   Dinners will be cooked on the line of march on the cookers and served on arrival at SEILLES.

8.   Men for demobilization will be paraded by Coys. and marched to Demobilization Camp on arrival at SEILLES at an hour to be notified later.

9.   Receipts for all stores handed over to the 1st South African Battn to be forwarded to D.C.R. by 2000 hours 14th inst.

10.   All billets to be left scrupulously clean.

11.   A reading of all meters (gas and electric) in billets will be taken and forwarded to D.C.R. by 0800 hours to-morrow, 14th inst.

                                        Captain and Adjutant.
                                        9th Battn. Manchester Regt.

Issued at 1200 hours by Runner.

Distribution :- Normal.

Vol 25

CONFIDENTIAL.

WAR DIARY

OF

9TH BN THE MANCHESTER REGT.

From 1ST to 31ST MARCH 1919 (ARMISTICE PERIOD)

VOLUME 5   No 3.

WAR DIARY
INTELLIGENCE SUMMARY

Army Form C. 2118.

1st Bn. The Cheshire Regt.

March 1919

Place	Date	Hour	Summary of Events and Information	Remarks and references to Appendices
SEILLES	1-3-19		Inspection of Billets by Commanding Officer, Inspection of men and lecture by Medical Officer. Sunday time will be used with us as 1st March 1919. At 2300 hours clocks and watches will be put on one hour.	
-do-	2-3-19		Joint C of E and Nonconformist Service in CERCLE HARMONIQUE, the services as usual. The C.O. regrets to announce the death of No.50099 Sgt. J.T.WIGHTMAN from Broncho Pneumonia whilst in the 50th CCS on 25th February 1919.	
-do-	3-3-19		Rifle meeting.	
-do-	4-3-19		Battalion took over the running of the Canadian Corps Concentration Camp.	
-do-	5-3-19		A draft under the command of Capt. C.D.WALKER of 5 Officers and 186 O.R. left by the 4.45 Army leave train for CALAIS for regulation to DUNKIRK where it will join the 1/6 Bn The CHESHIRE REGT. The draft consists of volunteers for the Army of Occupation and 1916 and after retainables men. Remaining Officers were Lt. S.E.GWINNELL, Lieut O.HAMILTON Lieut F. AITKEN-DAVIES, and Lieut J.M.RYAN.	
-do-	6-3-19		Concentration Camp Routine.	
-do-	7-3-19		4 Officers and 150 O.R. were sent off for demobilisation by L.S.D. train also 1 Lieut C.F. GROVES went with this party as a Platoon Commander conducting draft	

WAR DIARY
INTELLIGENCE SUMMARY.

of 9 Bn The Hampshire Regt

March 1919.

Army Form C. 2118.

Place	Date	Hour	Summary of Events and Information	Remarks and references to Appendices
SEILLES	8-3-19		Concentration Camp Routine. 6 Officers and 352 O.R. were sent off by L.S.D. train 8. Capt F.J. TAYLOR M.C. and Lieut N BANKS, having proceeded on demobilization are struck off with effect from 1-3-19.	Map LIEGE 1:100.000
—do—	9-3-19		Routine of Concentration Camp.	
—do—	10-3-19		—do—	
—do—	11-3-19		Lieut Col J.F.B. MORRELL, D.S.O, M.V.O, having taken over command of 199th Inf Bde (Brig Gen WILLIAMS. C.M.G, D.S.O, having proceeded to Staff College as a student) Major RN=E SCOTT M.C. taken over command of the Battalion.	
—do—	12-3-19		Routine of Concentration Camp.	
—do—	13-3-19		10 Officers and 565 O.R. were sent off by LSD train 13. Special Order of the day by Brig Gen. G.C. WILLIAMS. C.M.G. C.B.E. D.S.O. cmdg 199th Inf Bde. "On leaving the 199th Inf Bde I want to tell all ranks how hard I have found it to have commanded the Brigade for the last year. Thanks to the Courage and devotion to duty of all ranks, the Bn gained a great reputation in the fighting from SERAIN to SIVRY. To those who are going to the Army of Occupation I wish a long career and much promotion and hope they will carry on the good name of the Battalion. To those who are forming the Army of Occupation I wish every success in after life. To those who are returning to civil life I wish the best of luck and success in their migration and I know that the wonderful adaptitive and pluck shewn during the war will be kept in the days of peace.	

WAR DIARY / INTELLIGENCE SUMMARY

Army Form C. 2118.

March 1919   21st Bn. The Manchester Regt.

Place	Date	Hour	Summary of Events and Information	Remarks and references to Appendices
SEILLES	14-3-19		Concentration Camp Routine	
-do-	15-3-19		-do-	
-do-	16-3-19		-do-	
-do-	17-3-19		8 Officers (one of which was Lieut COLLENS, D.C.M. draft conducting) and 246 O.R. were sent off for demobilisation by L.S.D. train 17	
-do-	18-3-19		Concentration Camp Routine	
-do-	19-3-19		-do-	
-do-	20-3-19		Extract from LONDON GAZETTE no 31152 of 28-1-19. - The undermentioned have been mentioned in despatches of Sir G.F. MILNE, K.C.B, K.C.M.G, D.S.O, C in C, B.S.F of 1-11-18 for gallantry and devotion to duty. - Capt C.D.WALKER, Lieut & Qmr G. ILES, Capt Q.T.NEWMAN, and 2Lieut J. FAZACKERLEY, also 20162 6y 95Sgt (A/A) KAY, A.E. and 16 164170 Sgt NAYLOR.P. Extract from LONDON GAZETTE no 31151 of 25-1-19. - 2Lieut C.HILL to be Temp LIEUT 24-12-18 next below O.W.MITCHELL. 2Lieut O.HAMILTON to be LIEUT 1-2-19 LONDON GAZETTE 31231 of 21-2-19.	
-do-	21-3-19		3 Officers and 170 O.R. were sent off for demobilisation by L.S.D. train 21.	
-do-	22-3-19		199th Inf Brigade ceased to exist at 10.00 hours. Brigade Major proceeded to 66th Division.	
-do-	23-3-19		The train that should have run for demobilisation was cancelled owing to proposed railway etc strike in U.K.	

Army Form C. 2118.

WAR DIARY

INTELLIGENCE SUMMARY.
(Erase heading not required.)

9th Bn The Manchester Regt.

March 1919

Place	Date	Hour	Summary of Events and Information	Remarks and references to Appendices
SEILLES	24-3-19		Extract from D.R.O No 1464 dt 22-3-19 "Amendment":- The award of the "D.S.O" to Bt Major (T/Lieut Col) J. F.B. MORRELL, M.V.O. Commanding 9th Bn The Manchester Regt published in D.R.O. 1211, is amended to read "Bar to D.S.O". Authority M.S. to C in C No M.S 141/1996 dated 17-1-19.	Ct.Map LIEGE. 1:100,000
-do-	25-3-19		Concentration Camp Routine. The 66th Div will in future be known and referred to as 66 Div Cadre.	Attd
-do-	26-3-19		-do- Brig Gen A.J HUNTER, D.S.O, M.C. resumed command of 66th Div Cadre on 26-3-19.	Attd
-do-	27-3-19		8 Officers and 105 O.R also 8 Officers proceeding independently were sent off by demobilisation train L.S.D 24. 2nd Lieut J.W DAKIN proceeded for demobilisation with this party.	Attd
-do-	28-3-19		Extract from 66th Div R.O. "On giving up command of the Division on its reduction, I wish to thank all ranks for the hard work and high spirit by which they have put in and the spirit that they have always shown throughout the last twelve months. These qualities have enabled the Division to establish the reputation which it has gained for staff and these same qualities will stand every one of you in good stead throughout your lives. I wish you all God Speed and best of happiness and success in whatever you take up in the future.	Attd
-do-	29-3-19		14 Officers and 114 O.R. were sent off by demobilisation train L.S.D 29.	Attd
-do-	30-3-19		Concentration Camp Routine.	Attd

Army Form C. 2118.

WAR DIARY
INTELLIGENCE SUMMARY. 2/7th The Manchester Regt.

(Erase heading not required.)

Month: March 1919.

Place	Date	Hour	Summary of Events and Information	Remarks and references to Appendices
SEILLES	31-3-19		5 Officers and 116 O.R. were sent off for demobilisation by L.S.D. train. 3½ Bty. Capt & Adjt L.A. TURVEY, Lieut E. LEES, and Lieut C.H. BRABHAM left to join the 51st MANCHESTER REGT on the RHINE, 30-3-19. Effective strength (includes Cadre and men retained to run Canadian Corps Laundry at Camp) 6 Officers and 74 O.R. 1-4-19	Ref. Map LIEGE 1:100,000

B.A. Gallanger
Major
Cmdg 2/7 The Manchester Regt.

CONFIDENTIAL.

WAR DIARY.

OF

9th Bn. THE MANCHESTER REGT.

From 1st April 1919 To 30th April 1919. (Armistice Period)

Volume 5. No. 4.

Army Form C. 2118.

WAR DIARY
INTELLIGENCE SUMMARY. 9th Bn Manchester Regt
(Erase heading not required.)

April 1919

Instructions regarding War Diaries and Intelligence Summaries are contained in F.S. Regs., Part II. and the Staff Manual respectively. Title pages will be prepared in manuscript.

Place	Date	Hour	Summary of Events and Information	Remarks and references to Appendices
SEILLES	1-4-19 to 9-4-19		Concentration Camp Routine. 5 Officers and 161 O.R. for demobilisation were sent off by L.S.D. train 3. on 3-4-19. Lieut Col T.F.B MORRELL. M.V.O, D.S.O. returned from leave and resumed command of the Battalion and Lieutenant Col T.A. Collins. D.C.M. proceeded to join 6½ Manchester Regt. leaving 8.4.19. Concentration Camp 3-4-19. 2/Lieut COLLINS. D.C.M. proceeded to join 6/1 Manchester Regt. leaving 8.4.19.	Ref. Map W.S.G.E. 1:100,000.
-do-	9-4-19 to 16-4-19		10 Officers and 181 O.R. for demobilisation were sent by L.S.D. 10. train 10-4-19. Rev E.P RAITHBY C.F attached to the Battalion, proceeded for demobilisation independently 10-4-19. T/4/Capt F. RUDDY M.C, D.C.M. was appointed acting Adjutant vice T/Lt. Acting Adjutant LA TURVEY to 6/1 Bn Manchester Regt. with effect from 14-4-19. Rate of exchange for April for issue of cash to troops, France 3/4, Belgium 6 francs equals 3/7. 2/Lieut C.F. GROVES proceeded for demobilisation by L.S.D. 10 train 10-4-19. His Majesty The King has been pleased to approve of the award of the Albert Medal to No 1440 (Pte 2/Cpl) WILLIAM WHITEHEAD 9th Bn MANCHESTER REGT, in recognition of his gallant conduct in saving a comrade from drowning in the RIVER MEUSE on the 5th January 1919. 4 Officers and 150 O.R. for demobilisation were sent off by L.S.D. train 14 on the 14th inst. 2/Lieut W. BROWN 9th Bn MANCHESTER REGT. went included in this another draft conducting in 17-4-19 Demobilisation tram start from	
-do-	17-4-19 to up.		5 Officers and 341 O.R. for Demobilisation by a special train at SERAING Liege started from SEILLES now that the Demobilisation Camp at SERAING or LIEGE is closed.	

Army Form C. 2118.

WAR DIARY
or
INTELLIGENCE SUMMARY. 9th Bn. Manchester Regt.

April 1919.

(Erase heading not required.)

Place	Date	Hour	Summary of Events and Information	Remarks and references to Appendices
SEILLES	18.4.19 to 24.4.19		Major R.M.L. SCOTT M.C. proceeded to rejoin Cheshire Regiment, Chester, and was struck off the Effective Strength of the Battalion 22.4.1919. Captain R.W. BROWN. R.A.M.C (attached) proceeded to join 48th C.C.S. NAMUR and ceased to be attached 23.4.1919. Lieut. Colonel J.F.B. MORRELL M.V.O, T.S.O. proceeded on local leave to COLOGNE 23.4.1919. 3 Officers and 204 O.R. for demobilization were sent off by L.S.T. 24. train 24.4.1919. 5 Officers and 311 O.R. for demobilization were sent off by L.S.T. 26 train 26.4.1919. Lieut Colonel J.F.B. MORRELL M.V.O, T.S.O. Reported from local leave COLOGNE 26.4.1919.	Sketch Map. LIEGE 1:100,000
do.	25.4.19 to 30.4.19		Effective strength (excludes base and men retained to run Canadian Corps Concentration Camp) 6 Officers 69 O.R.	

J.F.B Morrell
LIEUT. COLONEL.
Commanding 9th Bn. Manchester Regiment.

1.5.1919.

15' CONFIDENTIAL

WAR DIARY

OF

9th BN. THE MANCHESTER REGT.

FROM 1st TO 15th MAY. 1919. (ARMISTICE PERIOD)

VOLUME 5. No. 5.

Army Form C. 2118.

WAR DIARY
or
INTELLIGENCE SUMMARY

(Erase heading not required.)

9th Bn. The Manchester Regt.

May 1919.

Place	Date	Hour	Summary of Events and Information	Remarks and references to Appendices
SEILLES	1.5.19 to 1.5.19		3 Officers and 193 O.R. for demobingation were sent off by L.S.II.1 train 1.5.1919. The Canadian Corps Concentration Camp ceased to exist under orders of O.C. 66th Divisional Reserve and this Battalion ceased to perform the duties of staff thereto. 2.5.1919. Battalion base operation order No.1 published. The Battalion came, Volunteers for Army of Occupation and retainable personnel proceeded by lorry from SEILLES to CINEY. 6.5.1919. 27 O.R. (retainable personnel and volunteers for the Army of Occupation) were transferred to the 1/5th Bn. Cheshire Regiment. They joined the 66th Division Jetaire Camp, CINEY 9.5.1919.	Ref. Map LIEGE 1:100,000
CINEY	8.5.19 to 15.5.19			

Army Form C. 2118.

WAR DIARY

INTELLIGENCE SUMMARY.

9th Bn. The Manchester Regt.

MAY. 1919.

(Erase heading not required.)

Place	Date	Hour	Summary of Events and Information	Remarks and references to Appendices

CINEY	8.5.19 to 15.5.19 (continued)		Bn. base consisting of Officers and other ranks 20 under, with Transport and Stores, proceeded by train from CINEY to ANTWERP EMBARKATION CAMP, ANTWERP, 9.5.19. Arriving ANTWERP at about 0630 hours 10.5.19.
			
			 Officer Commanding LIEUT. COLONEL. J.F.B. MORRELL. M.V.O.D.S.O.
			 Acting Adjutant CAPTAIN. F. RUDDY. M.C.D.C.M.
			 Quarter Master LIEUT. G. ILES.
			                          LIEUT. J.W. BENNETT. M.C.
			                             " C. HILL. M.C.
			                          2nd LIEUT. F.C. EGAN.
				Ref. Map. LIEGE. 1:100.000.

ANTWERP			Bn. other ranks 94. Bn. cadres left ANTWERP for TILBURY, England, dated 15.5.19. Personnel proceeded by S.S. 'SICILIAN' and Transport and Stores by S.S. 'KALIX', left TILBURY. BARROW 18.5.19.	

F.B. Morrell
LIEUT. COLONEL
9th Bn. Manchester Regiment.
Commanding 9th Bn. Manchester Regiment.

www.ingramcontent.com/pod-product-compliance
Lightning Source LLC
Chambersburg PA
CBHW080904230426

43664CB00016B/2723